Rabbit Food
Cookbook

Practical Vegan Recipes,
Food History, and Other Miscellany

Beth A. Barnett

SASQUATCH BOOKS
SEATTLE

Previous micro-editions published by Beth A. Barnett
© 11/2002, 10/2003, 03/2004, 12/2004, 7/2007 Beth Bee Books.
Printed in China
Published by Sasquatch Books
Distributed by PGW/Perseus
17 16 15 14 13 12 11   9 8 7 6 5 4 3 2 1

Cover design/illustration: Beth A. Barnett
Interior design/illustrations: Beth A. Barnett
Interior composition: Beth A. Barnett

Library of Congress Cataloging-in-Publication Data is available.
ISBN-13: 978-1-57061-811-6
ISBN-10: 1-57061-811-9

Sasquatch Books
119 South Main Street, Suite 400
Seattle, WA 98104
(206) 467-4300
www.sasquatchbooks.com
custserv@sasquatchbooks.com

CONTENTS

RECIPES

A Note About the Recipes

Vegans and strict vegetarians: This cookbook contains only strict vegetarian/vegan recipes with no animal derived ingredients—except for just a few mentions of honey, which, yes . . . is made by bees. The honey is very much optional and can be easily omitted or substituted with another sweetener.

Everyone Else: I know that not everyone using this book will be vegan or even completely vegetarian. This book will not self-destruct in protest. It's happy you're at least at the table! Welcome! Have a seat!

Please note: If you're not a strict vegan but you're cooking or baking to share with "vegans," leave out any honey, or ask first before using it. Many folks who will call themselves "vegan" will eat honey, but many will not. Also, it's best to check with your vegan friends or relatives about granulated sugar. If you're not sure how strict they are, try to use a sugar labeled as vegan from a health food grocery. Some sugar is processed through charcoal that is a by-product of the animal livestock industry. Most people who follow a vegan diet do eat "technically vegan" junk food now and then, so most won't turn away a treat with conventional sugar. But, it's still thoughtful to ask.

I absolutely hope y'all try *Rabbit Food*'s recipes for yourselves as written. I've tested and adapted the recipes for the ingredients I've listed, so I can't really speak to how they'll turn out with substitutions. But sure, yeah, I know—if your allergies/on-hand pantry supplies/preferences/whatevers dictate it, soy/grain milks and margarine can be replaced with their dairy equivalents.

Obviously, I hope you don't swap in animal products, but I won't be bossy about it. I already know it happens. Many of my friends and family aren't strict vegetarians, and I occasionally get enthusiastic reports of "I used your recipe!" that turn out to really mean, "I used your recipe but used butter and instant chicken gravy." If I wasn't pragmatic about these things, I would have gone crazy by now.

If you choose to substitute ingredients with some animal products, be it cow milk, butter, eggs, or even sausages, I hope you do so only sparingly and use farmer's market, local, organic, and free-range options for the sake of animal treatment, the environment, and your own health. Pretty please? If you need to be further persuaded in this recommendation, well . . . keep reading.   ★

Welcome to the New Edition!

Before *Rabbit Food Cookbook* became *this* book, it was a limited edition micro-press book I published in 2007 through my one-person micro-publishing business, Beth Bee Books. I am very proud of that edition of which I made 1000 copies, but I have to confess, it's complicated to be a one-person publisher. It's kind of nice to hand over the reigns to the folks at Sasquatch Books.

That wasn't the beginning of the story, though. Before the 2007 edition, there were four earlier version which we should really call fancy hardbound zines. I made to two to three hundred of those.

Earlier yet, while in college, it all started when I fashioned myself a small, quarter-page, three-ring book out of copy paper, with covers cut from the top of an Adriatico's Pizza box. Being an artist, I realized I needed to visually organize my favorite recipes to learn them better and use them more often. It helped, and my quirky illustrated recipe collection had its start.

Several more years have gone by since the most recent edition of the book, and in the meantime I've cooked and baked hundreds more times. I've learned some new tricks and I've even discovered new favorites! Given the opportunity to review and revise for this new edition, I have, of course!

This book has some new and updated information and quite a few new recipes about which I'm very exited! I've not removed any recipes, but I have made some changes here and there where I decided it was for the better. The philosophy of the recipes hasn't been changed. As always, I believe wholeheartedly in recipes that are practical, flavorful, and made from plants (and fungi, and a bit of optional honey). ★

Rabbit Food is Thinking Food!

Food and cooking do not exist in a vacuum. They are an integral part of our daily life tied to culture, ethics, environment, economics, and even politics. That is why although this is a recipe book, I have included some other things relating to the subject of food, such as gardening basics, sewing patterns, and food history. This shouldn't strike anyone as odd, since vegetarians think about food in a larger perspective. We make a deliberate choice to eat differently from and question a cultural norm of eating animals. We make choices and considerations beyond just the taste of food, or the simple presence of it. Whether or not a person chooses to strictly follow a vegetarian or vegan diet, taking the time and effort to think carefully about the impacts of one's food choices is a beneficial habit. For vegetarians, and especially for vegans, this isn't optional. It's pretty much unavoidable. We choose to care about, and think about, at least some of the implications of our food at every meal.

Just because vegetarians have more criteria for defining what is acceptable food to eat, that doesn't mean we are robotic, bland, freaks with no taste buds. Seriously. We all know that vegetarian, and especially, vegan food, gets dismissed as "rabbit food" by those who can only picture carrots and lettuce when they try to understand what a vegetarian would eat. Besides the very popular comment, "I just love [insert meat item here] too much," persons who are particularly unfamiliar with vegetarianism often ask that inane, "So what do you eat then, salad?" question, even though many familiar foods are already vegetarian or vegan in their usual forms. It makes me wonder what those people eat! Wow. Even many lacto-ovo vegetarians heavily reliant on dairy and egg products are unnecessarily stumped by vegan cookery.

This is all very silly. Anyone with an open mind and a well-rounded palate knows those folks are not thinking very hard, and they're quite uninformed! Really, the problem is the lack of imagination and variety in the diets *of the average person* with a meat-centered lifestyle, not an inadequate variety of vegetarian food.

Seriously, I'd rather be called a rabbit than eat that meat and dairy based diet, any day! A plant-based diet of "rabbit food" is a rich and varied cuisine based on fruits, vegetables, beans, grains, and nuts that non-vegetarians often eat too little of. Cooking and baking vegan "rabbit food" isn't even difficult. Without animal products at the center of one's plate, it's harder to get stuck in the rut of the typical and unhealthful American diet. Plant-based cooking leads us outward to incorporate recipes from around the world, though we can still find ways to make completely vegetarian versions of more mainstream American comfort foods (including desserts).

All of the recipes in *Rabbit Food* are made successfully without animal ingredients. You don't need to be a master chef to learn them: they are practical and every-day-friendly, not gourmet experiments. Who has time for that? I don't!

Many of the dishes are well-known as vegan staples, but none of this food requires a membership card for consumption! Vegan cookery is not just for dedicated vegans. Everyone else will benefit from eating foods without meat, eggs, cheese, or milk, even if he/she doesn't choose to adhere to an exclusively plant-based diet. Unless you've got an allergy to something in it, there's no reason to be wary of a vegan meal, or a vegan cookie (...unless you know the person who made it is a terrible cook, vegan or not!). I must say, I think the recipes in this book are delicious, and my dishes and desserts always receive compliments at parties!

Vegan dishes are typically much lower in fat (well, maybe excluding desserts which are about the same) and higher in fiber and antioxidants than meals with dairy, eggs, or meat/seafood. They contain (I think, healthier) vegetable rather than animal protein, and they have no cholesterol! Cholesterol forms naturally in your own body, but only animal foods contain the added cholesterol that most people also consume.

Besides the healthful benefits of vegan foods, there's an invaluable spiritual benefit of knowing that plant foods use fewer natural resources and energy, create less pollution, don't endanger ocean fish populations, and don't involve animal slaughter. For me, this is the biggest benefit—the icing on the (eggless) cake.

If vegan cookery is already part of your familiar, every-day lifestyle, that's lovely! Yay! I hope you can add these recipes to your favorites (I recommend you start with the breaded tofu)!

If you're not vegan or even vegetarian, you'll still be pleased by how tasty and satisfying these recipes are. Your vegetarian friends and family members will be impressed when you learn how to cook delicious vegan dishes and desserts! Your own mind, body, and spirit will likely be happier too! ★

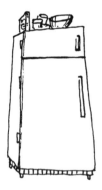

The Food Supply
in Perspective

Practicing a vegetarian or vegan diet requires awareness of food. Package labels must be read, questions must be asked. This heightened awareness and interest in food and the food industry leads vegetarians to demand food options that are healthier for themselves and more humane to animals and our ecosystem. We ask, "Where and what did this food come from? Did anything suffer?"

Voluntarily or not, we serve as ambassadors for an alternative way of living that suggests some of our society's norms are worth questioning and rejecting. There are few national surveys of vegetarianism, and their accuracy is not great, but with that in mind, probably 0.5–1% of Americans in the US self-report as vegan, around 3–10% identify as vegetarian, and as many as 10–20% are vegetarian-oriented. We're clearly a minority, yet some people find vegetarians and vegans very threatening. It's laughable that veganism, especially, can receive such grumpy, defensive reactions. Why aren't we simply ignored? 1%? Maybe we are hard to ignore. We lift the veil that others prefer not to look under. I think it's evidence that we ask worthwhile and difficult questions about the food supply, health, the environment, and animal welfare. We may be a minority, but we're slowly growing in number, and we're increasingly recognized as a valuable market of several million "foodies" who are passionate about how we spend our food dollars.

Sure, avoiding animal foods can be a challenge, but it gets easier over time with experience and knowledge. Food is ever-present, so vegetarianism requires self discipline and intention. It may begin with compassion for animals and concern for personal health, but often it reaches out beyond these things. Awareness of food issues can lead us to a better understanding of other social problems and injustices. Choosing a plant-based diet in our meat-obsessed culture is a daily practice of mindfulness and a rejection of denialism.

Our modern, industrialized food system has completely separated most people from the sources of their food, enabling a quiet ignorance of food, and animal foods in particular. At the beginning of the 21st century, The US has both an ever-growing population and record-high per capita meat consumption. The average national consumption equals about half a pound of flesh per person, per day. The huge quantities of cheap animal foods demanded by the population require the use of disturbing mass production practices. Sadly, it seems the average person would just rather not know about or confront this issue.

On the bright side, our modern food system also makes it evermore convenient and satisfying to be vegetarian today. The variety of vegetables, grains, herbs, and fruits available year-round in most communities around the country is impressive and unprecedented. We benefit from advanced production and distribution methods, rapid transportation, modern pasteurization and preservation, years of agricultural research, and a modern, diversified economy. Intentionally vegetarian, vegan, organic, and other "health food" products are experiencing robust sales and broadened markets.

There is greater awareness of vegetarianism in our society now than any time previously, yet most Americans still don't take the idea seriously, nor do they face the connections between diet, lifestyle, health, and happiness. An alarming portion of the population is plagued by poor health, contaminated and over-manipulated food supplies, lack of physical activity, environmental waste, and disconnected community structure. The news is filled with reports about our significant increase in diseases of "affluence"—heart disease, adult-onset diabetes, obesity, cancers, even depression. With nutrient enrichment and modern medicine we can fix most diseases and injuries that would have been fatal half a century ago, but now our population is sick from preventable diseases of a different sort. Vitamin enrichment, pills, and vaccines can't save us from our current, widespread health problems related largely to diet, lifestyle and unhealthful environmental factors.

Why do we spend so much of our GDP on healthcare for preventable health conditions? Suburbanization and poor urban planning have encouraged absolute dependence on automotive transportation for a large portion of Americans. Technology and industrial efficiencies have replaced many physical jobs with sedentary work. A variety of environmental, economic, and cultural factors have led to less physical exercise among children.

The bulk of our agriculture in the US has been chemical-dependent and environmentally unsustainable for decades. During production, agriculture and industry both continue to emit chemicals and particulate substances into the air, water, and food that often affect low-income communities the most. Many food products are polluted in a different way: they're full of sodium, refined carbohydrates (white flour, corn syrup, sugars), added fats, preservatives, and various chemical additives. High amounts of low-quality animal foods are also being consumed. Total food production has gone up, and prices have dropped, but our savings are artificial. The costs have simply shifted to healthcare expenses.

To meet the high demand for inexpensive animal foods, large livestock operations confine and crowd animals and feed or inject them with antibiotics and other pharmaceuticals. Animals are overfed and made grossly obese with grains and other substances that aren't natural or healthful for them. Producers are permitted to include rendered animal parts, including same-species parts of hogs and chickens, in livestock feed. They can also include the manure of animals, and even plastic pellets. Giant slaughterhouse operations move too fast to allow time for compassion or care in the killing of food animals. There *are* some small farms that feed, care for, slaughter their animals in a natural manner, but their meat, milk, and eggs aren't cheap, and they're not used in conventional packaged foods or restaurants. If a source doesn't specifically say cage-free, free-range, and vegetarian-fed, it's not reasonable to assume it is.

The profit-centered economic system of American industrial capitalism has been applied to our food supply, but nature doesn't respond well to industrialization. The industrialized model has become the norm after WWII, encouraged by government policy and capital investment, but now some conventional farm sectors just aren't profitable anymore and (ironically) rely on government subsidies. Organic farming is emerging as an alternative that is not just environmentally more sustainable, but also economically so.

Back when I became aware of the "normal" way of producing, selling, and consuming animal food in this country I was appalled and sought alternatives to make myself less complicit. I began by eliminating animal products from my diet. I still feel an incredibly valuable spiritual calmness knowing my choices don't support factory farming, and animals aren't killed to sustain me (well, except insects competing for plant crops). At first I thought I was completely in the clear, but over time, I have eventually begun to see that there are also important environmental and health problems associated with conventional crop agriculture and packaged foods. I still have ethical dilemmas to consider. Problems with conventional plant foods are not as glaring as the problems with seafood and animal livestock, but they're definitely important.

Unsustainable crop farming does damage to soil, air, and water resources and can even produce less nutritious food. Agricultural runoff—of chemical fertilizers, pesticides, animal wastes, and lost topsoil—is a major source of water pollution. This pollution has a lot to do with depleted soil and industrial, "conventional" farming practices. Animal foods require a huge amount of cultivated crops for livestock feed, and almost all of that feed is conventionally grown. Organic farming is much more accommodating and cooperative with the environment because it has to be. It comprises a small sector of the food supply, but it holds promise for weaning ourselves away from the mentality of the post-WWII industrial farming model. It has the potential to become a larger share of the food system. Organic options are not always available or affordable, but they're a better choice when you have the option to choose them.

My main food dilemma is between organic and conventional produce and grains, since I can't imagine taking the life of an animal at any time when I have plenty of other nutritious food available instead. This feels so completely obvious and normal, but, this is also because I am satisfied, healthy, and happy eating a pure vegetarian diet. It's not hard for me to leave out animal foods. Like most Americans, I live in a home with easy access to supermarkets and sufficient income to buy my choice of groceries. Desperate times may call for desperate measures, but we can prioritize certain choices when our lives are not desperate.

If anyone asked me about becoming vegan or vegetarian, I'd obviously say, "go for it!" A lot of people feel awesome when following a vegan diet, as in, "I've never felt better!" awesome, and it's an easy choice! It's not always clear why, but for some it's harder. Some people have inconvenient allergies; some get really grumpy if they can't eat any and every cupcake laid in front of them. Some folks want to continue to eat at least some animal foods. Okay. Should they bury their heads in the sand and eat factory-farmed meat, dairy and eggs, farmed salmon and overfished seafood?

It can be hard to accept that there is a middle ground if you've come to the conclusion that a plant based diet is an obvious option, but there *are* ways for those who decide to consume some animal foods to do so with compassion and ethics. I know some animal rights advocates feel absolute in their resolve against animals being used for food, but it's hard to disagree that any trend away from the industrialization of animals is still positive. For those who do choose to eat some animal flesh (or use eggs and dairy), choices are available that are significantly more ethically and environmentally sound than conventional animal products. Caring enough to be picky about which animal foods to eat or reject takes energy and self-discipline in its own right, though it's worth the extra effort for numerous reasons. I actually feel it's easier to just abstain—being truly judicious about animal food sources takes as much effort as pure vegetarianism. Local livestock, when raised by small growers under organic, cage-free, and free-range guidelines, is a far better alternative to the factory-produced and hormone-fed meat, eggs, and dairy that supply most food companies, groceries, and restaurants.

Conscientious farmers who are more concerned with their animals and the impact made by them than mass production outfits *do exist*. I am pleased to see the success of alternative livestock operations because they offer, for those who consume those foods, an option that has a lot more respect and understanding of animals kept or sacrificed for food. Of course, animals raised for food on these farms are still slaughtered. That's how it goes. But, an animal that lives its life free to move around and graze on its natural diet has had a much better life than one stressed and covered in manure in a cage eating crap. Animals brought into existence on our watch should not be subject to a miserable, painful life, and if we eat those animals or their eggs and milk, what are we putting in our own bodies? The "organic, free-range" alternatives cost more—a lot more—but, dammit, animal foods *should* cost more!

Cheap meat, dairy, and eggs should raise grave suspicions. The higher price of animal foods from conscientious farmers can be easily balanced by lower overall consumption of such foods, which is more healthful anyway. If consumed, animal foods should really be only a minor component of a mostly whole grain and vegetable based diet. Animal products have been awarded a starring role in

American cookery that is, I believe, undeserved, unhealthful, and irresponsible.

Our culture's obsession with meat and animal products is a widespread human tendency. In traditional societies, food animals are valued highly. In poverty, animal food is perceived as a ticket up and a sign of wealth, even though it becomes an abused luxury in affluent societies. Historically, and in many countries today without refrigeration and high-speed transportation, animal food is the only reliable source of important nutrients for some peoples at some times of the year. Animal foods are already expensive in impoverished places, with the exception of the fast food and snack food so common in America's poor communities. In comparison with the comforts of modern middle class life, in places where food is scarce, any and all calories are appreciated. Survival takes precedence. There are few self-professed vegetarians in hungry places, because even if the diet is primarily plant-based, the concentrated nutrition of animal protein is valued as energy-rich food. In the US, and other highly modernized societies, those of us who have the luxury to live above a survival mode have a relatively easy life. We have access to an incredible array of nutritious foods, year-round. With that luxury we have the ability and responsibility to be pickier about our food. We have the luxury not to turn to animal food to tide us over when nutrients are scarce, and to not support the ugly practices required to provide the volume of meat demanded by our society. Truly, to be healthy in the face of an overabundance of food, we have to have a different mindset about food than our struggling ancestors and peoples in less abundant societies.

Many Americans take food for granted and have little or no connection to its source. As a result, many people show little respect for our valuable soil or the animals that serve as food. We throw away an enormous amount of food and other resources every day. The discarding of wasted animal meat and other products is a colossal shame in light of the suffering and sacrifice of life that is made. Our land and animals, both domestic and wild, deserve our respect. We have a long way to go, but it is encouraging to see that more people in the US and elsewhere are trying healthier, less meat-centered foods, even if they are not committing to complete vegetarianism. Any increase in people caring about the state of our agriculture and food animals, and taking personal action, is hopeful. When it comes to food choices, individual actions make a difference.

Strict vegetarianism has become a normal, comfortable part of who I am, and a lifestyle choice I really enjoy. Broccoli, nutritional yeast, lentils, and tofu make me feel right at home. This plant-based diet has a foundation of nutritious, whole foods (despite occasional sugary treats, of course!), and it feels good physically and spiritually. Some new vegans claim they have more energy, their health conditions and mood have improved, or they've even rid themselves of diabetes and heart disease! I'm not a health expert, but I have been eating this way since I was a teenager, and I'm in good health and have plenty of energy . . . as long as I've had enough sleep! I think it's great that more people out there are giving it a try! Sure, not everyone is going to change to a completely vegan diet—people's lives and their choices are complicated. Becoming a person who is conscientious and picky about animal products, or becoming an "almost vegetarian" or and "almost vegan" is still very real progress.

When I was 16 and first read John Robbins's classic book, *Diet For a New America*, I soon ate my last chicken and cheese and hoped everyone I knew would be vegan someday. That hasn't come to pass, but I now hope more broadly that, over time, more people will learn and practice non-violent and compassionate values, and as a result greater justice and happiness can be spread farther in this world. It makes a difference, however small we may feel, to strive to live and teach values such as non-violence, empathy, compassion, and sustainability through our daily choices and actions—including our food choices—and to reject common tendencies of denialism and self-deception. When we hold ourselves accountable to these values, other animals, our environment, and our neighbors all benefit. ★

Health & Nutrition Considerations

Many people in our society who are convinced that meat and milk are necessary in human nutrition, dismiss vegetarianism, and believe that vegans, and even lacto-ovo vegetarians, are sickly and malnourished. This is an ideological argument and not a health-based argument. Sure, some vegans don't pay close attention to nutrition just like the average person doesn't, but I've found that vegans who want to follow a plant-based diet sustainably for the rest of their lives are quite interested in health and nutrition. A growing segment of vegans are following a plant-based diet primarily *because* of health and nutrition motivations. Health is very nuanced and personal, but it is clear that strict vegetarianism is not inherently unhealthful, and for many people it is a *more* healthful option.

In recent years, nutrition-based studies and trials with cancer, diabetes, and heart disease patients have shown remarkable health improvements for sick patients who switch to a vegan, plant-based, whole foods diet. By following a low-fat vegan diet, risks for many chronic diseases are lower to negligible compared with risk levels for folks who eat a typical American diet, or even a typical lacto-ovo vegetarian diet! Thanks to the work of doctors and researchers including Caldwell Esselstyn, James McDougall, T. Colin Campbell, and Dean Ornish, attitudes about veganism and health are changing. There are more open minds about this way of eating. There are numerous health-based books and programs available that focus on plant-based eating to heal or ameliorate chronic diseases and cancers.

Vegan diets are typically lower in fat, higher in fiber, and have no added cholesterol (because only animal produce it). Vegan diets are also completely dependent on plant protein instead of animal proteins which have been linked to greater cancer growth in animal studies and probably greater cancer risk in humans. Considering how the average American eats, it is *very, very possible* to be *much healthier* than the average American when following a vegan diet.

It is still important for someone following this diet to be mindful of nutrition. Just as many Americans eat with reckless disregard for health, so do some vegetarians and vegans. For example, there's a perception that vegans don't get enough calcium, but I have read that well over half of *all* Americans do not meet the recommended daily allowance for calcium. Vegans aren't exempt from this concern, although their chances of absorbing calcium from food is potentially higher than the general population. The moderate protein level in vegan diets leads to less interference with calcium absorption caused by protein.

Clearly, good nutrition cannot be assumed for *anyone*. Strict vegetarians and vegans must think about the nutrition of the foods they choose and eat a varied diet filled with more high-nutrition calories than "empty" ones. They must pay some attention to their intake of calcium, protein, and essential vitamins. A vegan diet based on french fries, sugary beverages, and white flour is not a healthy diet!

People choose a strict plant-based diet for various reasons: environment, compassion for animals, health, its relative convenience in cities, even weight loss. Such a diet can be very healthful, sustainable, and satisfying for a lifetime; however, yes, I have met quite a few vegans, especially teenagers and young adults, who ignore their health completely. It's not likely these folks will be vegan long-term if health is not a consideration. Even if the sole motivation for being vegan is for animal rights and welfare, an unhealthy idealist isn't going to be a very effective or motivated activist for these beliefs for long. It's just not sustainable. Nutrition matters.

Whatever one's motivation and level of commitment to vegetarianism, it is important for everyone to pay attention to his/her body, and be aware of changes. It is uncommon but not impossible for teenagers and adults to develop or discover new allergies to wheat gluten or soy products. It's a real bummer if this happens after committing to a vegetarian or vegan diet. This kind of development can drastically change what foods are options in an already restricted diet and may require a person to reevaluate the boundaries of his or her diet. Some folks do manage to follow a gluten-free or soy-free vegan diet, but that's definitely more of a challenge.

A healthy diet and stable body weight are good forms of "preventative medicine." Vitamin supplements can help round off the edges of an imperfect daily diet and relieve worrying about intake of specific vitamins. I personally try to balance more laborious meal preparation from whole food ingredients with some fortified convenience products and occasional vitamin supplements. This works for me, and is more practical for busy people than obsessing over achieving a 100% organic and from-scratch whole foods vegan diet. Besides, sometimes the organic apple on display was shipped all the way from Chile, while the conventional one is from just the next state over . . .

There are several nutrients important for everyone that also require some attention in a vegan or nearly vegan diet: protein, calcium, vitamin B-12, omega-3 fatty acids, and fiber. All of these are found in many plant foods, but it is best to become aware of good sources that you enjoy eating and make sure to eat those foods regularly. The good news is that it isn't very difficult to get these nutrients if food is varied and healthful.

Protein: Your body uses proteins to build muscle and aid in the function of many organs. If you eat varied and nutritious plant-based foods you should get sufficient protein! Yay! Many whole foods already have 10–50% of their calories in protein. Plus, many people who eat animal products consume far more protein than they need. Getting about 10% of our calories from protein is suitable for optimal health. The US Recommended Daily Allowance is weight-specific: 0.8 grams per 1 kg of body weight per day. 1 pound = 0.45359237kg, so to get your personal RDA, do this: your weight in pounds x 0.4535927 x 0.8. A 120 lb person's RDA will calculate to 43.2g/day, and a 200 lb person's calculates to 72g/day. The amount of protein needed is also affected by age, size/gender, and level of activity. More active people should take in more protein.

Even if you think protein isn't something to worry over, it is true that high-protein foods can be more filling, ensure sufficient protein intake, and should probably be a component of a vegan diet. Good sources of protein include tofu, wheat gluten, spinach, beans, and nuts. Grains also contain significant protein. Veggie-meat products like "salami," soy burgers, and vegan jerky are tasty high-protein sources. The better choices are those products made with grains, tofu, and wheat gluten rather than those heavily composed of soy protein isolate or concentrate. Energy bars like Clif and Luna bars are also good sources for protein and a number of other nutrients, including B-12. Adding soy, hemp, and pea protein powder to foods is also an option.

Calcium: This nutrient is very important for teeth, bones, metabolism, the nervous system, etc. Some vegans are deficient in calcium, but so are the majority of Americans! Sure, calcium is provided by milk products, but that source also comes with a lot of milk protein, which inhibits calcium absorption. Plant sources of calcium are better, and some research has shown that individuals who follow diets with lower animal protein and lower calcium have less risk of osteoporosis.

I find it easiest to boost calcium intake by using enriched soymilk and other nut and grain "milks," eating broccoli and spinach fairly regularly, and taking an occasional multivitamin with calcium and/or a calcium-magnesium or calcium-vitamin D supplement.

Vitamin B-12: The main source for this nutrient is animal foods because the bacteria that produce it live in the soil and in animals' digestive tracts. B-12 can be absorbed by organic produce from healthy, living soil, but only in small amounts. In the past, and in less developed parts of the world, B-12 also has been consumed by people directly from soil, mostly because of less sanitized conditions. In the US our produce is either santized for us before we buy it, or we have the ability to wash it well (which is good for a number of other reasons), so as an alternative to eating dirt, or animal products, vegans should take B-12 supplements occasionally. Our bodies store B-12 for a long time, but it is important to keep this nutrient in mind for long-term veganism. Some nutritional yeast is fortified with B-12, and some enriched soymilks have it added, as do vegetarian multi-vitamins. Look for vegetarian B-12 supplement lozenges that dissolve under the tongue, for best absorption.

Omega-3 fatty acids: These supposedly help prevent heart disease, which vegans are less likely to develop anyway. Ha! But we still benefit from these nutrients. Fish and fish-oil are usually mentioned as a source, but Omega-3s are also found in plant foods like flaxseed, tofu, and avocados—no fish required!

Dietary Fiber: Generally speaking, a vegan diet is naturally high in dietary fiber. Fiber is the tougher part of plants' cell walls, and it's good for us to eat, even though we can't digest it. Toxins tend to attach themselves to fiber and get out of your dietary system faster that way. If you're eating a vegan diet, then you're on the right track, but it is still possible to fill your diet with too many overprocessed grain products that have been stripped of their fiber altogether. It's best to try to choose whole grains when you can. If you eat a lot of fruits, vegetables, and whole grains, you'll be set.

Exercise: Um, okay, this isn't a "nutrient" or actually in food at all, but physical exercise is essential for good health, for everyone. Physical activity gets your blood circulating, and most importantly, it sends blood to your brain! You can't sit down and eat it, but exercise is just as important as good food. Fortunately there are endless different ways to get it. If you go outside in the sun, you'll even get more of the essential nutrient Vitamin D.

Food is a fundamental part of our lives, and our beliefs and values are reflected in the foods we choose to eat. Importantly, when we strive to treat other animals and our ecosystems better through our dietary choices, we must not forget to treat our own bodies well too! ★

For more reading on nutrition & food choices:

Campbell, T. Colin and Thomas M. Campbell. 2006. *The China Study: Startling Implications for Diet, Weight Loss, and Long-Term Health*. Dallas: Ben Bella Books.

Nesle, Marion. 2006. *What to Eat*. New York: North Point Press.

Robbins, John. 1987. *Diet For a New America: How Your Food Choices Affect Your Health, Happiness, and the Future of Life on Earth*. Walpole, NH: Stillpoint Publishing

Robbins, John. 2011. *The Food Revolution: How Your Diet Can Help Save Your Life and Our World*. San Francisco: Canari Press.

Report of the Dietary Guidelines Advisory Committee on the Dietary Guidelines for Americans, 2010. Washington, DC: US Dept. Ag. Available from the USDA website http://www.cnpp.usda.gov/dgas2010-dgacreport.htm

Wasserman, Debra and Reed Mangels. 1991. *Simply Vegan: Quick Vegetarian Meals*. Baltimore: The Vegetarian Resource Group.

Vegan Outreach, www.veganoutreach.org, www.veganhealth.org

The Industrialization of Food in America
– a Handy Timeline

Enormous changes have occurred in the American diet over time. Most doctors and nutritionists agree that a large portion of the contemporary American diet is unhealthful and contributes to heart disease, diabetes, overweight, and other health problems. One cannot assume that our predecessors had perfect diets, but they certainly were more physically active, they were more trim, on average, and they ate mostly whole, unprocessed foods. Many Americans of the past ate fewer calories. The food landscape was much different.

Today, in the United States, food is everywhere. The instant availability of ready-to-eat snack foods and the sheer volume and variety of food at supermarkets would be mind boggling to our ancestors, and it is mystifying to many contemporary people from other countries of the world. When it comes to food, we live like kings. Every day can be an occasion for a feast, if we wish it. This food is relatively inexpensive for Americans—the average portion of household income spent on food is under 10%, though it's 19–25% for our low income households (USDA). Compared with the rest of the world, our food costs are low.

With such great access to food, one would think Americans should be healthy and happy, with no issues of food scarcity or malnutrition, but of course, this is not the case. Much of the food available in this country is highly processed and stripped of nutrients. Our cheapest and most ubiquitous foods are full of sugar, fats, refined grains, and industrially produced dairy, egg, and meat products. Many Americans eat mainly these things and suffer the health consequences, yet don't understand or appreciate the connection between their food and their health. Ironically, billions of dollars in subsidies are paid by the US government to producers of corn (and therefore high fructose corn syrup and corn-fed livestock), soybeans (also used mostly for livestock feed), wheat (milled into white flour), and (white) rice—key components of much of our cheap, low-quality, processed, and genetically modified foods.

The industrialization of foods occurred because of changes in agriculture and processing technology, population growth, social change and urbanization, and a shift from a subsistence-centered to a market-centered food economy. Although industrialization and modernization of our food sector has led to a giant and cheap supply of unhealthful food, it hasn't been all bad. I would not suggest a return to the 18th or 19th century. Great innovations and efficiencies have come along that have made life easier for all of us, and especially women. The modern conveniences of our food system have freed women to spend less time on their traditional role of food preparation. Truly, while our modern food system has its flaws and makes it easy to be unhealthy, it also makes it easier than ever to be very healthy! Much more food is available year-round than ever before, including healthful grains and vegetables that have originated from all corners of the world. It is also easier than ever to eat a well-balanced, pure vegetarian diet.

One major issue that industrialization and modernization has caused in our relationship with food is disconnection. Throughout history, plants and animals used for food and farming have been revered. They have had sacred importance. Today, the disconnection of the average American from the source of his or her food has become highly dysfunctional. One step toward healing this problem is to re-learn about our food. It is useful and intriguing to understand how we moved from a nation of mostly rural farmers, dependent on the weather and closely tied to animals and the land, to a nation of mostly suburbanites/urbanites who shop in enormous food warehouses, think very little of the animals and crops that make up their food, and rarely, if ever, cook from fresh, whole foods. Let's consider how that happened with a little trip through recent American history . . .

Indigenous, before European Influence:

The diverse native peoples living in North America practice various levels of agriculture for both subsistence and trade. Some groups are primarily nomadic, hunting game and gathering wild, edible plants. Coastal populations fish and gather oysters and clams where they are accessible. Others practice limited, yet sufficient agriculture in river floodplains. Some harvest wild rice, others grow maize crops. It is common for different peoples to trade to improve their access to food. Long before their contact with Europeans during the European "Age of Exploration," North American peoples develop  agriculture without the use of the wheel, and without domesticated "beasts of burden." They lack iron and steel—stronger materials used in Europe and Asia in agriculture and weaponry. The limited power to plow and clear land and lack of wheeled carts to move materials restrict the scope of native agriculture. The absence of horses and wheels holds back the volume of trade between populations on the continent.

1600s & 1700s Colonial/ Revolutionary:

When Europeans arrive in North America, they encounter many successful civilizations and settlements with well-fed peoples living on the foods available from the land. In some cases, New England pioneers soon take over the villages and cultivated fields of native peoples devastated by European diseases, against which they had no immunity. The European colonists learn to cultivate maize from locals, but as their settlements grow they stop cooperating and begin to take Indian lands farther inland. Brutal and sometimes lengthy "Indian Wars" occur on the frontier of European settlements through the 17th–19th centuries. In many cases, entire cultures are destroyed by a combination of war and imported diseases. Despite adopting some local crops and practices, in general, rather than learn from the well-adapted ways of the local cultures, the Europeans import their economic beliefs, social structures, and food crops/agriculture to the colonies. A combination of slaves, indentured servants, tenant farmers, and small yeomen work the land to produce food and cash crops.

When the United States is established, between 5% and 10% of its people live in cities. At least 90% of adults make their living in the agricultural economy. Enslaved labor is widespread: Northern farmers commonly own one or two slaves; Southern plantations own hundreds. British industrialization begins in the 18th century, and it uses the colonies as a source of raw materials to supply its factories. American society remains rural and agricultural because of the frontier of cheap land (taken from indigenous people) and because of legal limitations on manufacturing and industry, enforced by Britain.

Other areas that later become part of the United States are first claimed by Spain and France. Until the United States buys or annexes the land these areas are typically less dominated by European immigrants and retain their native autonomy. However, indigenous agriculture and food traditions begin to break down as these peoples are assaulted and disrupted by policies of the US Government which favor the endless waves of new settlers over the indigenous peoples.

Immigrants to the colonies come from a variety of European countries and bring their own food traditions with them. There is no refrigeration other than that which occurs naturally in winter and the cooler temperatures provided by cellars. Foods are cooked over a fire in the home, or in a brick oven. Salting, smoking, drying, home canning or potting, and pickling are methods used to preserve foods, and these techniques have been in use around the world for thousands of years.

Late 1700s—Early 1800s: Cut from Northern lakes, ice begins to be used to extend the season for some foods and to extend the use and storage of perishables. Ice is primarily used in Northern areas in the summer, but some ice reaches the south to be used in plantation icehouses. Ice is also used to preserve fish caught on the

37

coasts and sent inland up the rivers. Household iceboxes come into use in the 1830s.

Produce and meats are available in cities and towns at open air market stands. Foods are local and seasonal, mostly because land transportation is slow. Restaurants that exist are located in inns and hotels. There is a large market for wild birds and game. The Louisiana Purchase land acquisition in 1803 opens the Midwest and Plains areas to settlement and farming by European-origin people. Native peoples are often killed, displaced, or removed to other regions to make way for Midwestern agriculture.

I8I5: The first cookstove is introduced. It will gradually replace cooking over an open fire in large fireplaces or outside. The cooking heat is still  generated by burning wood or coal, but the fire is more efficient and produces less smoke. The stove is adopted by wealthier classes widely by the 1830s; for poorer classes cooking over fire is common until after the Civil War.

I830s—I840s: A movement for "social uplift" develops and includes a new consciousness of health. This is a time of many grassroots social movements including women's suffrage, anti-slavery, temperance, and religious revivals. Concern over gluttony and overeating is met with a call for moderation and the consumption of wholesome, plain foods. Food faddists abstain from spices, alcohol, meat, sugar, coffee. Vegetarian eating is advocated by Sylvester Graham and the Kelloggs, among others. Cold cereals are popularized and marketed as health foods.

I840s—I860s: "Canning" using metal materials rather than ceramic pots is developed in Europe and imported to the US. Early canning focuses on oysters and sardines. Condensed milk is first developed in the 1850s, as is modern baking powder. Canned foods are popular, though expensive, in far-west "frontier" settlements. Male-dominated mining towns depend on canned goods for variety in their diets. Households begin to keep store-bought canned foods as a back-up to use when fresh produce and meat are unavailable. Glass "Mason" jars are invented in the 1850s and become popular for home canning—replacing tin and ceramics.

I846—I850: After the Mexican American war (1846–48) ends, the US takes approximately half of Mexico's lands including California, Arizona, New Mexico, western Texas, and parts of Nevada, Utah, and Colorado. The eastern part of Texas, independent from Mexico since 1836, is annexed by the US. The southwest contains a combination of Spanish-speaking peoples and native peoples with a different staple diet from the Anglo population. The

 diet of "white" Americans at this time is heavily influenced by British and German heritage. In this period migration from Ireland intensifies as tens of thousands flee from the devastation of the Irish potato famine.

1860—1870: Sales of canned foods increase 600%!

1861—1865 Civil War: Military mobilization boosts demand for canned foods and Borden's new condensed milk product. The war boosts both industrialization and urbanization in the North. Southern plantations are eventually forced to shift their agriculture from cash crops to food production as supplies from the North are cut off. Northern armies are fed by ongoing food production in the Midwest and Northeast. The great demand for canned goods provides the capital needed for canning companies to expand inland to the Midwest. More vegetables and fruits are canned than had been before.

Late 1860s: Urbanization of the population continues to increase, along with railroad construction. Several national brands of prepared foods emerge and may be found at general stores around the nation and its territories. These companies mass-produce baking powder, dry

breakfast cereals, flavoring extracts for baking, gelatin, cooking fat, yeast foam, milled flours, oats, and coffee. General stores also begin to sell several types of crackers and dry biscuits in bulk. Chicago and St. Louis emerge as centers of meat packing for the growing cattle industry,

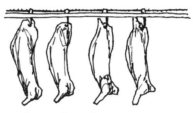

benefiting from the railroad expansion, southwestern rangelands, and demand for meat in the more populated East.

1869: The first trans-continental railroad line is completed, linking California to the East Coast. Now, fruits and  vegetables can be transported from the West Coast more easily, extending the availability of warm-weather produce into the winter.

1870s–1880s: Prices for many basic food products drop significantly due to transportation and manufacturing innovations. Prices for beef, coffee, lard, flour, rice, sugar, milk, beans, and tea all decrease. Sugar prices fall

because of improved refining technology and intense competition. Cheap prices shift consumers away from the use of sorghum molasses toward refined, white sugar.

Around half of the US population lives in cities. The unlimited and gratuitous hunting of wild animals, especially birds, through previous decades has caused major population declines and some species extinction. Buffalo on the Plains are slaughtered in great numbers, shot from railroad cars. Slaughtering the buffalo herds weakens the wide-ranging Plains Indians and clears the land for fenced cattle ranges. The refrigerated train car is invented in 1871 and leads to the consolidation of large, centralized slaughterhouse operations, and small operations are pushed out of business.

Margarine is invented and patented in the early 1870s. It is slowly accepted as a butter alternative, but not without some initial resistance.

1880s: Butter and cheese-making, activities previously carried out by women to bring cash into farm households, begin to shift out of the home, replaced by industrial manufacturing processes. Tropical fruits like pineapple and bananas become regular imports to Eastern markets. Department stores are established and begin to offer ready-to-wear manufactured clothing. Ready-made clothing places new emphasis on the idea of average body weight and size, causing new difficulties for persons outside of those ranges.

I880s—I890s: Wheat milling is increasingly industrialized. Small local millers are replaced by large corporations that use new processing technologies, including steel rollers in place of stones, to grind and separate flour from bran. White flour, though much less nutritious than whole wheat, becomes popular, since it is lighter, more refined, and has long been available only to the wealthy. A major trend toward the use of white flour gains momentum, though white flour doesn't become the majority type used until after 1900.

Also in this decade the cafeteria style restaurant is invented, and Campbell's canned soups are introduced in 1897.

I890s—I930s: There is a shift away from open markets and general stores to more specialized neighborhood groceries, butcheries, and bakeries. These stores begin as small, independent entities—but soon some of these grocers begin to expand, buying out other stores,

 setting the foundation for larger supermarket chains. New pastimes related to radio, film, automobiles, and other new technologies draw family members away from home-based activities, making quicker meal preparation desirable.

1900s–1910s: Concern over canning, slaughterhouses, and questionable or adulterated ingredients leads to passage of the 1906 Meat Inspection Act and Pure Food and Drug Act, which takes effect in 1907. These laws initiate government inspection of food and drugs where it did not exist before. Young women find urban jobs, drawing them away from the home. Middle class families hire fewer live-in cooks and choose to cook more for themselves. Manufactured bread from commercial bakeries begins to sell in cities, although most women prefer to make bread at home themselves. Urban immigrants with poor housing and limited kitchens buy many of the emerging commercial foods. The first electric refrigerators are mass-produced in 1913, but are only accessible to the wealthy. A new manufacturing process for crimping lids onto tin cans increases production capability from 1,500 cans per day to 35,000 cans per day and cuts out the jobs of skilled lid-soldering craftsmen.

During WWI, American farmers greatly increase cropland under production to meet demand from war-torn

European nations. The surplus of demand keeps prices high, and farmers have the credit and profits to invest in new technologies and land improvements.

1920s: The US population is recorded at 106 million in the 1920 census. The prohibition of alcohol begins in 1920, although household wine-making is still permitted. A liberalization of women's roles includes a drastic change in women's clothing. Loose and more revealing clothes provide freedom of movement, but also make women more conscious of their bodies. Magazines and journals that discussed the problem of "underweight" in the Victorian Era now focus on the problem of "overweight." Canned, prepared baby food products are introduced  and become popular. The candy business booms with candy bars, ice-cream bars, and other candies selling in corner shops. Food processing companies General Foods and Standard Brands buy up smaller processors and dominate the processed foods market.

With the end of WWI, agricultural prices fall as Europe requires fewer imports of food from the States. The expansion of the previous decade turns into a liability of excess production and lingering debts. These factors quickly cause a farm depression.

45

I930s: Agriculture shifts further toward the industrial model of large, commercial farms. Many family farmers lose their land and leases in the depressed economy, facilitating consolidation by stronger players. Rural farmers increase specialization in single crops and grow less of their own food. Farmers become less self-sufficient, purchasing more of their personal food supplies from grocers in town. Ironically, while unemployed workers go hungry in the cities, farmers destroy surplus crops, attempting to improve prices.

The electric refrigerator gains accessibility, slowly replacing iceboxes. Icehouses of New England begin to go out of business.

The grocery shopping cart is invented in 1937. The cart complements self-service grocery aisles, the refrigerator, and the automobile to encourage larger purchases of food at one time, and fewer trips to the market.

I940s: The lack of nutrients in refined white flour worries doctors and public health officials enough that in 1941 the US Department of Agriculture begins to require the enrichment of white flour and white breads with several basic water-soluble nutrients lost through the refining process.

New manufacturing machines are invented to cut, peel, and cook foods in bulk for canned and frozen food products. During WWII (1941–44), the American military demands huge quantities of pre-packaged and prepared foods for rations. Huge government contracts enrich the largest food processing companies, ensuring their dominance after the war. The agricultural economy recovers from the depression, but the trend toward conglomeration and agribusiness is set.

Late 1940s–1950s: The refrigerator is now a fixture in the kitchens of all but the poorest households. Large commercial freezers and refrigerators also become affordable, allowing grocery stores to display and stock large amounts of frozen foods. Through the 1950s the frozen food industry develops and expands rapidly.

Chemical companies create about 400 new chemical additives for use in processing foods. The additives are used to simulate/replace taste, texture, and color lost from foods in processing.

Agriculture is also affected by new developments in chemistry. A broad array of pesticides, herbicides, and fertilizers are encouraged for use in farming. The increase in land productivity seems miraculous, and the shift toward chemical farming is given the name "the Green Revolution."

Poultry farmers begin adding antibiotics to chicken feed in 1950 allowing for a ten-fold increase in density within chicken barns. Chickens become a much more affordable source of meat, and the use of

antibiotics is quickly transferred to other livestock industries for similar purposes.

With the rise of suburbs and the end of war rationing
and industrial restrictions, supermarkets are built in the
new outlying neighborhoods. Large companies that began
as small grocers grow to compete in regional markets. In
this period, accompanying the interstate highway con-
struction boom, fast food restaurants are opened, their
business model is developed further, and they soon grow
into large regional and nation-
al chains. The population of
the United States in 1950 is
approximately 151 million.

I960s: Rachel Carson's

1962 book Silent Spring warns against the dangerous
and alarming side-effects of the agricultural and household chemicals now in widespread use. Some
farmers and consumers begin to question
the assumptions, and safety, of the "Green
Revolution." In the growing counter-culture
movement, there is interest in a return to
whole foods and farming, including a back-to-
the-land movement.

Special "diet foods" are created and
become a separate niche in the processed
foods market. The first low-calorie soft drinks
are introduced, including Tab Cola and Diet

Pepsi. Other indications of Americans' interest in weight control include the introduction of sugarless gum and the establishment of Weight Watchers.

I970s–I980s: The 1970 Census shows the population has reached 203 million.

The first low-calorie beer, Miller Lite, is introduced in 1974—another response to calorie-counting. Diet soft drinks become more popular after the introduction of Aspartame sweetener in 1983.

As food processing escalates, the alternate movement toward whole, fresh foods and vegetarian foods also continues to develop as a niche market. These foods are found in small food co-ops and specialty health food stores and are largely absent from other groceries and supermarkets. Organic farming quietly regains some popularity as an alternative to agriculture dominated by chemical pesticides and fertilizers since the late 1940s.

The microwave oven, invented in the late 1950s becomes economical and popular by the late 1970s and early 1980s. This new cooking method leads to new processed food products designed specifically for use in the microwave.

A process for mass production of high fructose corn syrup is developed in the early 1970s, and by the mid-1970s it begins to be used in soda beverages and other processed foods.

49

1990s: "Nutritional Facts" information becomes mandatory on food labels in 1994. The nutrition table shows calories, fat, protein, sugars, fiber, and some other nutri-

ents, as a supplement to the list of ingredients. Scientific and anecdotal studies on health and nutrition are popular topics in the media, yet they often provide conflicting advice. Meanwhile, rates of adult-onset diabetes increase by 40% from just the previous decade, and both overweight and obesity increase among American adults and children. A 1999 study by the Center for Science and the Public Interest finds that the average person gets 9% of his/her daily calories from soda—a three-fold increase since 1978. Americans consume an amount of soda beverages equal to 600 cans per person, per year. The consumption of sugar by children and adolescents continues to increase—especially through soft drinks and fruit-flavored juice drinks.

Fat "substitute" products are introduced by food scientists to boost the low-fat processed foods market. Proctor & Gamble's Olestra fat substitute is introduced in snack chips in 1998. The substance is welcomed cautiously, as it causes gastrointestinal discomfort in some consumers.

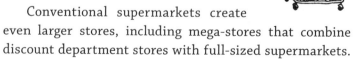

Conventional supermarkets create even larger stores, including mega-stores that combine discount department stores with full-sized supermarkets.

Beginning in the late 1980s and escalating in the 1990s, US fast food chains become multinational and export their restaurants to countries all over the world.

A significant shift begins to take place in the health food and whole foods market, and the demand for processed and prepared health foods and organic foods expands year after year. Toward the end of the decade, some of the more successful health food stores begin to buy out others, creating new supermarket-sized natural food grocery stores. The variety, quality, and availability of low-fat and vegetarian processed food products increase significantly. Some smaller health food co-ops and shops close due to competitive pressures from larger stores.

At this same time, genetically modified (GM) crops become widespread. The most advanced genetic manipulations of crops include insertion and exchange of cross-species, and even cross-kingdom DNA genes. Pesticide attributes are incorporated into crops. Chemical, biotech, and food corporations patent seeds and engineered plants and collect royalties. By the end of the decade, the majority (over 70%) of non-organic processed food products contain some GM ingredients, yet they are not labeled.

2000s to present: The food industry spends $25 billion a year on advertising—mostly for snack foods, fast foods, and other processed convenience foods. Only 2% of advertising is for fruits and vegetables. Adult obesity rates in the US have doubled from the 1960s.

Use of high fructose corn syrup, introduced in the 1970s, has increased from zero to over 80 pounds per capita in the US in 2000, while cane and beet sugar use has actually decreased. In total, per capita use of caloric sweeteners is up by 40% since the 1950s, and the estimated average consumption of sugars is about 32 teaspoons per person, per day in the US. The USDA's recommendation is not more than 10 teaspoons per day in a 2,000 calorie per day diet.

A handful of corporations dominate the grain trade and food products industries. In the past decade the organic and natural processed foods sector has grown further, but in tandem with this growth, the giant food companies now own the majority of the natural foods brands.

Despite the interest in health food and vegetarian eating among a minority of Americans, per capita meat consumption has significantly increased in the past 50 years. We have the impression that Americans ate more meat, historically, but that isn't really the case. Total animal flesh consumed per person per year average in 1950 was 138.2 pounds, and in the 2000–2010 decade it fluctuates between 201–210 pounds per person: a 50% increase! That's over half a pound of meat, fish, and or

poultry per person per day. Some of this food is wasted and not eaten, but the animals have been slaughtered just the same. Based on the average weight of food animals, this includes the slaughter of around 40 million cattle, 9 billion chickens, 240 million turkeys, and 120 million hogs per year. The majority of these animals are raised in part or completely in industrial scale operations called Confined Animal Feeding Operations (CAFOs). Only a small percent of the animal food supply is from grazing and free-ranging animals. Most cattle graze, but then finish up in a CAFO.

The 2010 census records the US population at over 308 million. Fewer than 2% of people in the United States are now employed in agriculture. Each year hundreds of small family farms are sold to larger corporate farms or to developers, and fewer Americans enter the farming profession, largely because so much of it is dominated by prohibitively expensive industrial-scale farming. 80% of Americans now live in large cities and their suburbs and do not play any part in growing their own food. On the hopeful side, the organic food sector is one of the only domestic agricultural sectors experiencing real growth and profits. It is still possible to be a successful small farmer, but more likely if the farm is organic.

*   *   *   *   *

Huge changes have occurred in the food supply and in our relationship to food since the start of the industrial era. In the past, food was simpler. It was almost all local. There was no such thing as agribusiness, processed food companies, packaged food, or transgenic crops. It is possible to have that kind of pre-industrial relationship with food—many people in the less developed parts of the world still do, and a few Americans intentionally choose to as well. But, for most of us, that's not feasible. The majority of us don't live on farms, and we rely on others to raise our food, so we eat the food that is for sale in the marketplace. The addition of industrial efficiencies and modernization to our food supply is really a mixed bag of good and bad results, with quite a few unintended consequences. Overall health improved in the industrial era with the advent of canning, enrichment, frozen foods, and faster transportation. More food variety is available to everyone year-round. There is less food scarcity in the population, and more calories are available. On a survival level, we're better off, and with the right choices, we can be very healthy and happy. It's the overzealous overreach of industrialization that plagues us, not beneficial innovations in pasteurization and fresh food preservation that allow us flash-frozen fresh fruits and vegetables year-round.

Though the vast majority of us now do not spend our days farming the food that sustains us, it is in our best interest not to be apathetic about our food or our food system. It is, and always has been, beneficial to understand and respect the food that we rely on for our health and sustenance. To not pay attention is a dangerous choice. We do have a choice to take the good things that we gain from modernization and use them to eat better, and to eat more compassionately. We have a choice to be informed about what we eat. It's up to us to have the will power to care, and act accordingly.   ★

Sources, and Further Reading, Viewing, and Watching

Farrell, Chris and Daniel Zwerdling. "Who Bought the Farm." American Radio Works radio documentary, 2002.

Hooker, Richard. *Food and Drink in America*. Indianapolis: Bobbs-Merill Co, 1981.

Hurt, R. Douglas. *American Agriculture: A Brief History*. Ames: Iowa State Univ. Press, 1994.

Kenner, Robert, Dir. *Food, Inc.* documentary film. 94 min., 2008.

Levenstein, Harvey. *Paradox of Plenty*. New York: Oxford University Press, 1993.

Levenstein, Harvey. *Revolution at the Table*. New York: Oxford University Press, 1989.

Nesle, Marion. *Food Politics*. Berkeley: Univ. of California Press, 2002.

O'Connor, Amy. "White lies about white flour." *Vegetarian Times* magazine. August, 1996.

Olver, Lynne, Ed. The Food Timeline. 1999–2011. www.foodtimeline.org

Roberts, Paul. *The End of Food*. Boston: Mariner Books, 2009.

Sapkota, A.R., L.Y. Lefferts, S. Mackenzie, & P. Walker. 2007. "What do we feed to food production animals? A review of animal ingredients and their potential impacts on human health." Environmental Health Perspectives, 115 (5):663–670.

Schlosser, Eric. *Fast Food Nation*. New York: Perennial, 2001.

Schwartz, Hillel. *Never Satisfied: A Cultural History of Diets, Fantasy, and Fat*. New York: Free Press, 1986.

Sowell, Thomas. *Conquests and Cultures*. New York: Basic Books, 1998.

Spurlock, Morgan, Dir. *Supersize Me*. documentary film, 100 min., 2004.

Stacey, Michelle. *Consumed: Why Americans Love, Hate, and Fear Food*. New York: Simon & Schuster, 1994.

Staten, Vince. *Can You Trust a Tomato in January?* New York: Simon & Schuster, 1994.

Thomas, Antory. *PBS Frontline. Fat*. WGBH Boston/Frontline. documentary film, 1998.

US Department of Agriculture. *Agriculture Fact Book 2001–2002*, "Chapter 2 Profiling Food Consumption in America." Washington DC: US Gov. Printing Office, 2002.

Wight, Heather. Jan. 25, 2011. "The History and Processes of Milling: Impacts on Nutrition and Local Grain Systems." College of the Atlantic HUM Journal. www.humjournal.com.

Woolf, Aaron, Dir. *King Corn*. documentary film, 88 min., 2007.

First Garden

Gardening, even in simple and limited practice, can be very fulfilling. It can connect you to the vegetables and fruits you eat more intimately than your usual produce aisle. It's kind of magical. It tunes your thought toward nature and the progress of the seasons. If you're a city person, and it's likely you are, growing your own vegetables certainly gives you a better appreciation of farming and the people who still make a profession of growing crops. You'd be in a sorry place without them.

In a clay pot or garden bed you can watch the life cycles of those amazing plants that produce tasty things. You can get to know your favorite vegetables better. Gardening is easier in a yard or community plot, but it is possible anywhere that there is good sunlight and a person who can remember to add water.

I was initially intimidated by gardening because the books I picked up for instruction seemed to make a big ordeal out of every step. Gardening seemed too complicated with lots of room for failure. Then my mom told me to stop fretting and just try putting some seeds and starter plants in some dirt, water them, and see what happens. What did I really have to lose? To be honest, my first attempt wasn't particularly successful or bountiful, but it did get me started! We must remember that vegetable gardening is really miniature farming—something that can be very technical. It is self-defeating to intend to become an expert the first few times you have a garden. Start simple and step up your fussing and complexity gradually.

I'd say I am nowhere close to being a gardening expert, but each year I am a little more helpful and knowledgeable when asked for advice. In the meantime, I can offer some easy tips for those less in-the-know than myself.

If you've never grown anything before, give it a try!

Sprouting From Seeds in Pots:
Start early (around February) to begin growing plants from seeds. The earlier you begin, the bigger the starter plants will be by the planting season. Seeds need warmth and moisture before they can germinate.

I. Some seeds transplant well and need to be sprouted in the window sill first. Others do best planted directly into the dirt where they will stay. Read the seed packet and/or a gardening reference.

2. In the early spring, or earlier, put your seeds in nutritious potting soil or mature compost mixed with dirt, in a small terra cotta pot that has been soaked in water, or in a peat starter pot. You can also use left-over tofu tubs or (soy) yogurt containers with holes in the bottom for drainage. It's okay to put a few seeds in one container.

3. Plant your seeds to the correct depth (indicated on seed packet) and water them well with warm water. Cover the containers with plastic wrap and place them under a lamp, in a sunny windowsill, or in a gas oven that's off but has a pilot light on (warmer than other places usually).

4. Wait.

5. Keep watering with warm water. Unless the seeds are duds, they should sprout eventually. Sprouting may take a few days or a couple of weeks.

6. When the seeds sprout, put them in a place with light, but keep them warm and covered.

7. Once you have sturdy seedlings, transplant the best ones into slightly larger pots or other containers so each has its own container.

8. Keep transplanting into larger pots

or into the garden outside, once the weather is warm enough. Again, the seed packet will indicate the planting time. If you have numerous different plants, mark reminders on a calendar for their different planting times.

Preparing Your Garden Plots:

Ask yourself a few questions: What parts of the yard get the most sun in the day? Can you dig up grass if you have to? Is your house old? Is it possible that the yard is contaminated with lead paint chips, automotive products, or household chemicals?

If you have good reason to suspect contaminated soil in your yard, plan to make raised beds, or plant in big pots, with dirt and soil from somewhere else. Your vegetables could potentially suck up metals and other toxins if their roots are in bad soil, and then you would eat them. Some state agricultural extension services offer free soil testing for contaminants and nutrient levels.

Pick a spot that has worms and keeps some moisture, if possible. Is the existing soil clayey? Or is it sandy? Was anything growing in the chosen patch of dirt before? If weeds thrive there, you may have better luck with your plants. Choose a place away from the canopy and root systems of trees that gets several good hours of sun each day. It can't hurt to add some potting/gardening soil and compost to the dirt that you have, because it might be sapped of nutrients. Buy a few bags of organic soil mix and shovel them into your garden dirt. Dig down at least 1.5 feet and turn the soil. Rake the garden plot down so it is even, and then make some rows for plants.

Before you plant, plan the general organization of the space. There are often sections in gardening books that say what plants are good to plant next to one another. Plant the starter plants and seeds according to their instructions on their packaging. Plant things you like to eat! Keep in mind that some vegetables like tomatoes and corn have deep roots while others, like lettuce, are fairly shallow. Plant accordingly.

Smaller varieties of tomatoes and other popular vegetables are available in seed catalogs, for those who are determined container gardeners. Also, choose deeper containers for larger plants and shallower containers for short ones. The expected height of a plant is related to the expected root depth. Line wooden containers with plastic, and fill with a soil mix.

Pay attention to the weather as spring progresses. Some vegetables, like lettuce, do well in the cooler spring. Plants that thrive in the heat of the summer, such as peppers and tomatoes will not do much out there in the garden if you plant them too soon. In some cases, garden stores will have tomatoes and peppers for sale earlier in the season than the time best for planting. The first warm days of spring will make you want to start your garden! You'll excitedly buy a pack of pepper starts in Oregon in early May and plant them right away! You'll sadly watch them not grow very much. Trust me, I've done this several times. The gardening season is different depending on what part of the country you live in, so you'll have to find some local references to guide you. Plant seed packets almost always have their US map with climate zones to help you. Resist the temptation to plant your hot weather vegetables and fruits outside too early.

Watering & Mulching:

It is better to water at the roots or base of the plants rather than from above. Water regularly, deeply and thoroughly, to promote strong, deep roots. You will need to water more often in the hottest and driest part of the summer.

A good mulch will help your soil retain moisture, so you have to water less. Plus, it helps to keep weeds out of the spaces between your plants. Mulch a few weeks after transplanting your plants, when they are moderately sized and won't be overwhelmed by the added material. Hay is a good mulching material, as it is cheap and will eventually decompose and enrich your soil. Grass clippings saved from mowing make an easy and even cheaper mulch. Keep a pile handy by your compost area.

Garden Clean-Up and Composting:

In the fall, when first frost is forecast, remove the remaining vegetables or fruits that you can salvage. Some of them, like tomatoes, can ripen while sitting inside on the window sill. When frost comes and your garden is spent, remove the plants and put them on your compost pile, unless they are diseased. Turn the soil in the plot and add mulching grass or hay, or even fallen leaves. If you're especially ambitious, sprinkle clover seeds on the soil to make a nitrogen-rich cover to feed the soil for the next spring.

If you have room to keep an active compost pile in your yard, you can make your own supply of rich soil for your garden. You don't need a fancy composting contraption, though that will save you space and will look more tidy if your space is limited. What your compost pile needs is your kitchen's plant-based food waste, water, and bulky yard clippings, such as dead leaves, mowed grass clippings, hay, or even shredded newspaper, and the right worms.

Throughout the year, add your kitchen cuttings, grass and yard cuttings, and turn them together occasionally. Turn under and cover any new food waste added to the pile. Avoid putting pulled weeds in your compost, espe-cially those that have gone to seed. You can easily end up with more weeds! Finally, the worms make all the difference! Redworms, also called "red wigglers" will love, love, love to eat all of your food scraps, even your moldy, rotten food, and quickly! It is unlikely that they are already living in your garden, so you may have to buy/adopt some. Redworms are redder, thinner, and shorter than earthworms. They're available for purchase by mailorder, and through some garden stores and bait shops. When I learned about redworms and started to see them in action, I was amazed at the difference they made. They're fabulous, really.

Perennial Herbs:

Most of the vegetables we eat are annuals and require new seeds each spring or summer, but many herbs we use to season them are perennials and can be planted just once and simply trimmed and maintained! A little $3 seedling from the garden store can turn into a mature and reliable herb plant in your garden for years afterward. Easy perennial herbs for a novice gardener are (upright) rosemary, oregano, and mint. Rosemary and oregano will do well in containers or even in your decorative landscaping. In many places rosemary will stay green through the winter. Oregano will become dormant in winter and needs to be trimmed back before spring. Mint comes in many varieties and does very well in containers with ample space. It will die off and return in the spring. It's best to keep mint confined—if you plant it in your garden it might take over like a weed! Of course, as with all gardening, the behavior of these plants will depend on the climate of your region, so look for some local resources on how they'll behave where you live.

Now you're ready to get started! Watching seedlings grow in the windowsill through spring is a great way to prepare for summer! It feels good to watch the plants progress, and they require much less energy and responsibility than pets and children! By gardening and raising plants, we also cultivate our ancient and intimate connection to soil and the foods we eat. Although most of us don't live on farms, it is good for us to keep this connection alive. Philosophical reasons aside, everyone knows fresh ripe tomatoes off the vine are better than any supermarket offering, and supplementing home cooking with food you brought up from seed is empowering, cost-saving, and convenient!

Remember, if your first try isn't amazing, don't get discouraged. Gardening takes some practice and experience. It is always a learning experience—but that's what makes it interesting. If something fails the first time, just try again! ★

grocery bag

Taking your own bags when you shop for groceries is a very easy way to be conservation-minded and reduce waste. It's even better when your bags are awesome, and it's easy to make your own to be sure of that.

This pattern is really easy, especially if you have a sewing machine! All you need to cut out is a rectangle and two strips of webbing! Fold 'em up a bit, pin, and sew! Simple! If you hand-sew this it will take a lot longer, but it's totally do-able. Make sure to make strong stitches and use thicker thread.

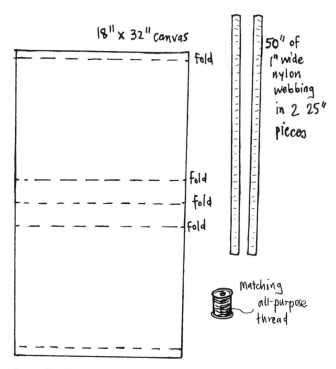

18" x 32" canvas

fold

50" of 1" wide nylon webbing in 2 25" pieces

fold

fold

fold

Matching all-purpose thread

Materials:

⌘ 18 inch x 32 inch rectangle of canvas or other strong material (try colors, or patterned fabric!)

⌘ Matching all-purpose thread

⌘ 50 inches of synthetic (or cotton) 1 inch strap webbing, cut into two 25 inch sections

⌘ Sewing machine, or extra time and a needle

⌘ Straight pins

⌘ Ruler or flexible measuring tape

Instructions:

I. After choosing your canvas, or some fabulously pat-terned, sturdy fabric, cut the material to a 18 inch x 32 inch rectangle. Cut the webbing straps into two 25 inch lengths. Fuse the frayed ends of the nylon webbing by melting them very slightly with a lighter or match. It doesn't take much heat. You can also use cotton webbing for the straps, but don't put a match to that!

2. Fold the fabric in half, right-side-out, and put one pin in each side, at 2½ inches up from the center fold.

3. Now fold the fabric back the other way, wrong-side-out, and pin down along the sides to the part you pinned before. Re-pin the bottom 2½ inches so that the pins run through all four layers. You should now have 3 folds at the bottom of the bag. (Try turning the bag right-side out to look at your progress. There should be a triangular corner showing at the bottom

of both sides, with a flat, rectangular bottom. Don't forget to turn the bag wrong-side-out again when you're finished looking.)

4. Sew two seams (for strength) along the left and right pinned edges of the fabric at approximately ¼ inch and ½ inch from the fabric edge.

5. Remove pins.

6. With the bag still wrong-side-out, fold down and pin the top opening by one inch toward the wrong side, all the way around. For a more finished edge, fold the opening down by 1½ inches instead, and fold the last half inch under again, to hide the unfinished edge of the material. Pin in place.

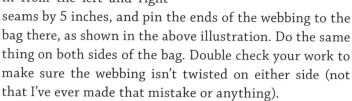

7. Next, pin the webbing straps into place. Measure in from the left and right seams by 5 inches, and pin the ends of the webbing to the bag there, as shown in the above illustration. Do the same thing on both sides of the bag. Double check your work to make sure the webbing isn't twisted on either side (not that I've ever made that mistake or anything).

8. Finish the hem for the top opening of the bag: sew all the way around the top opening ¼ inch or less from the top fold. Double-stitch over the webbing straps for reinforcement. Sew a second seam close to the bottom of the hem, all the way around, reinforcing the webbing once again (and hiding the cut edge, if you folded it under by the extra half an inch).

9. Remove all remaining pins, fold the bag right-side-out, and go shopping!

produce bag

So, you've tackled the grocery bag and you're ready for more! Reusable produce bags have been making an appearance in more stores lately, although buying a stockpile of them becomes pretty expensive. They're handy and reduce the need to use thin plastic produce bags.

Reusable, breathable bags are great for potatoes, yams, peelable fruit, and other not-so-moist veggies like peppers, broccoli, etc. I do avoid using them for storage of leafy greens and celery since both can dry out in a breathable bag, and I usually store these for a while in the fridge before I use them up. They're great for storing potatoes, though!

Bags made from polyester netting will be less susceptible to staining by sludgy, neglected old vegetables and will be transparent enough for your checker at the store to see through. For a natural fiber option, thin cotton muslin is a nice (though opaque) alternate.

Now on to the how-to:

Materials:

⌘ 14 inch x 35 inch rectangle of fine polyester no-see-um/ mosquito netting (preferable), petticoat netting (won't be as fine a mesh), or thin cotton muslin (opaque and natural fiber).

⌘ Matching all-purpose nylon-coated thread

⌘ 58 inches of ⅛ inch round, braided polyester cord, cut into two 29 inch pieces (or cotton ⅛ in cord)

⌘ Sewing machine with universal 80/12 general-purpose needle (or extra time and a hand-sewing needle)

⌘ Straight pins

⌘ Ruler or flexible measuring tape

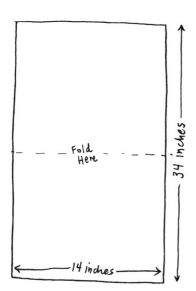

Instructions:

I. Cut out your fabric of choice. The 14 x 34 in. size I recommend will result in a 13 x 15¾ inch finished bag. The dimensions can be changed, but follow the same hemming instructions and dimensions.

2. Fold the fabric in half as shown. (Mesh fabric won't have a wrong and right side, but if you're using something with a printed

"outside" you need to fold your rectangle "inside-out.")

3. Pin the left and right sides together, stopping 2¼ inches from the top opening of the bag. Mark this with a straight pin or pencil so the measurement is clear.

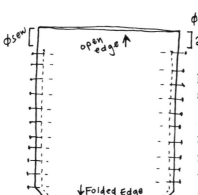

3. Snip the bottom corners just a bit to allow for a more rounded bottom to the finished bag (optional).

4. With a medium length straight stitch, sew up both sides ½ inch in from the edge, stopping at the mark 2¼ inches from the top opening. Double back on ends of these stitches.

4. Remove pins.

5. Fold the top opening down by 1⅛ inches to the outside/wrong-side of the bag. Pin in place.

6. Turn the bag and flatten out the side seam's selvage edges. Make sure this is folded in where you're leaving an opening edge for the draw strings. Repeat on the other side.

7. Sew around the entire top opening at about 1 inch from the folded edge. You will have openings on both sides of the bag for drawstrings.

8. Remove pins and turn bag right-side-out.

9. Cut the ⅛ inch cord into two equal 29 inch long pieces if you haven't already done so.

10. Thread the first cord through one side, all the way around past the other opening, and back out the same side. Use a safety pin to assist you to feed the end through the hem if necessary. Tie the ends together in a knot close to the edge of the bag.

11. Repeat the last step from the other side with the other piece of cord. The two cords form two loops that are oriented in opposite directions.

12. With a lighter or match, very briefly heat the ends of the cut polyester cord to prevent fraying. Don't do this if you're using cotton cord!

13. Test your work! Pull the drawstrings closed. Voila!

SALT   PEPPER

INGREDIENT
TIPS In case you don't already know...

Applesauce

is useful in vegan baking to add bulky moisture in place of eggs, or even oil. It comes in various forms, but for cooking and baking look for unsweetened Applesauce. If you're not likely to eat a whole jar otherwise, buy a 6-pack snack pack. You can open just a small amount at a time, and you won't have moldy applesauce in the back of your fridge. Yep. I have often had left over moldy applesauce in my fridge . . .

Baking powder

is an essential leavening ingredient to get baked goods to rise. It contains an acid and a base that react when moisture is added. I suggest an aluminum-free and double acting variety. Make sure yours is fresh, or at the very least, not expired! It makes a huge difference. Trust me.

To test whether your stash is any good, place 1 tsp in a juice glass, and add about ¼ cup of hot tap water. You should get a vigorous, bubbling reaction. Exposure to moisture will deactivate baking powder over time, so remember to never dip in wet spoons, and keep your container sealed air tight.

Baking soda is only the base chemical (sodium bicarbonate) found in baking powder. It reacts when it is mixed with an acid such as vinegar, lemon juice, etc.

Beans

Most dry beans need to be pre-soaked overnight or quick-soaked for an hour, then pre-cooked. I rarely have the patience to plan ahead in this way, especially if all I want is a cup and a half of beans, so for pre-soak beans I always call for canned beans. Fresh-cooked dry beans are cheaper, they may taste a bit firmer and fresher, and they can be cooked and frozen for use later so that they're easier to use on a whim. See page 88 for specific information about cooking dry beans!

Canned beans are good, though! They come in salty water, but the sodium can be reduced significantly by straining and rinsing the beans before use. To replace the can's liquid, add ½ to ⅔ cup water. One 15-ounce can of beans contains about 1½ cups of pre-cooked beans.

Bragg Liquid Aminos

All Purpose Seasoning is a health food store staple and is also found in health food aisles of grocery stores, if they know what's up. I consider Bragg's to be a seasoning sort of like tamari/soy sauce, but much milder. It adds subtle flavor and isn't as salty. It is good on broccoli, rice, added to veggie burgers, etc.

Egg Replacers

Eggs? Nah. Baked goods often use eggs as a binder, but

most can be made with something else instead. There are several options, and sometimes it depends on the rest of the recipe how well each will work.

★ **Ener-G Egg Replacer.** This is a dry, powdery substance, mostly composed of tapioca flour and potato starch, that comes in a yellow box. You whisk 1½ tsp with 2 Tbs water for each "egg" substitute, to help cookies and cakes to rise. It works well in many, but not all recipes. It will also keep in your pantry for years at a time. For best results, though, make sure your supply has not expired. It's widely available at health food stores and some supermarkets. I've been using it for many years!

Tip: To obtain a gooey texture, mix in warm water gradually with a small spoon or mini-whisk, then heat a few seconds at a time in the microwave until the starch begins to congeal.

★ **Ground Flax.** For each "egg," grind 1 Tbs flax seeds in a clean spice/coffee grinder and then mix this with 3 Tbs warm water in a blender or food processor.

Flax is an excellent substitute for egg, but it provides a more "nutty" flavor than Ener-G's Egg Replacer. It's best in spice cakes, quick breads, pancakes, and waffles, and serves as a source of omega-3 fatty acids.

Flax seeds lose nutritional value over time once they has been ground, so it's best to buy them whole and grind them yourself.

★ **Bob's Red Mill Egg Replacer.** Bob's product is made mostly of soy flour and gluten flour. It will keep longer if you store it in the fridge.

To replace one "egg," mix 1 Tbs of the powder with 3 Tbs of water. Bob's product seems to work well where Ener-G or Flax would also.

★ **Soy Flour.** If you don't have an egg replacer product, mix 1 Tbs soy flour with 2 Tbs water for each "egg"—best for cookie situations.

★ **Silken Tofu.** For one "egg," blend up ¼ cup. Try this replacement in recipes that are too crispy or dry with powder+water substitutes.

★ **Soy Yogurt.** This is a very similar option to the silken tofu. Use a scant ¼ cup plain soy yogurt for each egg replacement.

★ **Fruit Puree.** ¼ cup of fruit, such as applesauce or mashed banana can substitute for egg and/or oil, but this will add fruity flavor. Since that may change the nature of the cookies or cake, I don't suggest using fruit in place of eggs haphazardly.

Grain & Nut Milks

In addition to soymilk, there are several milk alternatives made from grains and nuts, such as rice, oat, coconut, almond, hazelnut, and hemp. Each has its own flavor. Using these interchangeably is easy but will result in differing flavor undertones in recipes. Also, for example, soymilk is thicker and can be curdled in a way that rice milk cannot, so in some cases the properties of these "milks" are also variable. Feel free to experiment, but you might find that the texture outcomes in cooking and baking also differ.

Honey

is an insect product, and, yes, it is an animal product, and insects are part of the Animal Kingdom. There is, however, variation on how it is viewed by strict vegetarians/vegans who otherwise avoid any foods made of or by animals. If you personally use honey, be sure to check before using it when cooking for someone who identifies him or herself as vegan, and leave it out if you're taking a dish to serve as a vegan option at an event or party. By pure definition, honey is not vegan; however, it is also true that exponentially more insects are harmed and intentionally killed in farming, even in organic farming, to provide us with viable plant foods. Everyone draws his or her line somewhere, so, I have included honey in a few recipes, but always as optional.

Honey is available as a local product in most areas, and those same honeybees play an essential role in pollination of regional flowering food crops. Honey is commonly favored as a sweetener for whole grain breads by both commercial-scale and small bakeries. It has antimicrobial and medicinal qualities that soothe inflamed tissue, such as a sore throat, so it is good for use in hot tea.

Margarine

Though cholesterol-free, traditionally margarine has been created by hydrogenating vegetable oil, which forms trans-fats. Recent research on trans-fats is leading to health concerns, so the industry has started changing how it makes margarine. There are now many non-hydrogenated margarines available! Not all of these are dairy-free, so check the labels.

Earth Balance is a vegan margarine with organic ingredients and no hydrogenation. Soy-based and non-soy versions are available. It works just as well in recipes as other traditional hard margarines.

Nutritional Yeast

is a great ingredient for gravies and breading. Nutritional yeast is yellow and flakey and has a salty, slightly cheesy flavor. It is usually rich in vitamin B-12 (if it was grown on an enriched medium). Keep some in a spice shaker with a few cups on hand.

Poultry Seasoning

Don't worry, this contains no animals! It is actually a mixture of spices traditionally used on poultry. It includes sage, pepper, coriander, thyme, savory, and allspice. Use it on tofu, tempeh, and seitan to get a traditionally "chickeny" flavor. Tasty, and essential!

Quinoa

is a nutritious and tasty whole grain—if you prepare it correctly! Left unrinsed, it is bitter and unpalatable. Its short cooking time is comparable to short-grain white rice. See page 91 for instructions to cook it just right.

Salt/Sodium

Salts are needed by our bodies, but in only moderate amounts. Too much sodium can trigger headaches, water retention, and hypertension, so, while cooking it is important to consider the ingredients used that already include sodium before adding additional salt!

Try to use unsalted or low-salt vegetable bouillon and reduced salt canned beans, if you can find them. Straining and rinsing canned beans will also significantly reduce sodium content. If a recipe calls for a whole can of beans with the liquid, but you choose to rinse your beans, add ½ to ⅔ cup of water.

It's best to only add table salt a little at a time. It's hard to undo your mistake if you over-salt your dish! If you know you tend to like foods salty, when cooking for others hold back a bit and allow for adjusting salt at the table.

Seitan

is a high-protein meat-substitute made from wheat gluten. It is chewier and more "meat-like" than tofu and tempeh. Seitan substitutes well in the role meat plays in many dishes, and it can be made easily from scratch!

Soymilk

is a versatile milk substitute. It's available in unrefrigerated aseptic boxes or in refrigerated milk cartons. In some areas local companies produce and sell soymilk too!

Not all soymilk tastes the same, so try several to find your favorite. Take some time to find a variety available in your area that is suitable for cooking. I find Silk's recently "new and improved" Original flavor to be too sweet for anything but sweet desserts and coffee. Trader Joe's Original is less sweet. Vanilla flavor works in some breakfast and dessert recipes, but stick with a plain, original, or even unsweetened flavor for cooking main dishes.

Try several brands until you find one you prefer. Aseptic pack varieties often say to "shake well" because separation can occur. This is annoying, but not an indication that the soymilk has gone bad. Refrigerated carton varieties tend not to have this issue. Regardless of the brand you like best, there's no reason to think you have to love it straight, by the glass.

Soymilk Powder

Mostly, I use powdered soymilk in my to-go hot cocoa, or to add extra richness in baking. My favorite is Better Than Milk vanilla. It's good to keep some on hand for "oh no, we're out of soymilk!" baking emergencies, although fresh soymilk is preferable.

Soy Protein Powder

doesn't really taste like anything. It is, however, a useful addition to breads, smoothies, oatmeal, cookies, etc., to boost protein content.

Tamari

A form of soy sauce, tamari is made from fermented soybeans, whereas soy sauce also usually contains wheat. Look for a low-sodium option: it tastes about the same and is better for you. I tend to find tamari in health food sections rather than in regular grocery stores by the soy sauce. Anyway, soy sauce can be substituted for tamari in recipes if necessary.

Tempeh

is a fermented soybean cake and a good protein source. It can also be made from other fermented beans and grains. Hands down, it has best results when it is marinated or cooked long enough to absorb other flavors.

Sometimes tempeh is sold pre-steamed. If it hasn't been steamed, make sure to steam or boil it for 20 minutes. A tip: to improve flavor and digestibility, even if the tempeh has been pre-steamed, first steam it or simmer it for 10–15 minutes in water or vegetable broth at a low boil, and then drain the water. Following steaming and cooling, a quick marinade will add flavor dimensions. Tempeh can be kept frozen without a noticeable change in the texture, which is a definite plus. If you buy it to cook "sometime soon," and not immediately, you'll be glad you froze it.

Tofu

Soybean cake, a.k.a. tofu, comes in more than one form! Unless the recipe mentions "silken," you probably want **extra firm**. Big difference! Silken tofu has the texture of custard and is good for pies, puddings, and sauces. Firm tofu is what you stir-fry. It holds its form.

Not all "firm" tofu is alike! Try different brands to find the firmest available in your area. Firm tofu made regionally and sold in bulk is often the best choice. Another place to look for good firm tofu is Asian groceries, where it may be cheaper than at health food stores (though likely non-organic).

Fresh tofu should have a nutty, clean smell, and once a package is opened, the tofu needs to be stored submerged in water in the fridge. To keep it for a few days, the water needs to be changed every day or two. When tofu goes bad it smells rancid, like spoiled milk and can become slimy. Freezing tofu is an option, but this will give it a new texture. Once thawed, frozen tofu is very spongy and chewier than regular refrigerated tofu.

TVP

Textured Vegetable Protein (TVP) is sold dry and in bulk. It is in a lot of vegetarian convenience meals and it's a popular addition to vegetarian chili. This product is high in protein and serves as a meat substitution in some recipes, though it should be used only occasionally, as it contains a small amount of naturally occurring monosodium glutamate (MSG). Folks sensitive to MSG should probably leave out this ingredient. TVP has to be hydrated with warm water for about 5–10 minutes before use.

Vegan Mayo

can be made from a recipe but it is much easier to buy it ready-made. Unlike traditional mayonnaise, vegan options lack eggs and contain blended tofu. There are three brands I know of available, Nasoya "Nayonaise," Hain "Vegenaise," and Trader Joe's eggless mayonnaise. I think Nayonaise is more like Miracle Whip and Vegenaise is more comparable to traditional mayo. I use Nayonaise myself, and it is almost always available at health food stores or in well-stocked health-food aisles of conventional groceries. You might try vegan mayonnaise substitutes even if you aren't vegan because they are a bit safer and much lower in fat than traditional mayonnaise.

Vegetable Bouillon/Stock

can be made from scratch from a mix of typical soup veggies, herbs, and a little oil, in water, boiled. It is convenient to store it in 1–2 cup servings in the freezer for use as needed. Stock is also sold in ready-made form.

Bouillon cubes are my default because they require less preparation and can be used to make instant stock by dissolving them into hot water. Vegetable bouillon also comes in powder and concentrate forms.

It is very important to notice that some ready-made cubes and pastes come with quite a lot of salt in them, and some have no salt at all. Read the labels!

I have written my recipes for use with no-salt bouillon because this allows control of the salt level and its timing. If you only have salted bouillon on hand, make sure to rinse any canned beans well before use and exclude any additional salt. Preferably, find or make unsalted bouillon.

Wheat Flour

Most of us learn to bake with refined white flour and have to teach ourselves how and when to use whole wheat. It can't be substituted in all recipes, though whole wheat pastry flour (less dense than standard whole wheat flour) will perform quite well in many cakes and cookies. Since whole wheat is so much more nutritious, I highly recommend that you give it a try. In breads, such as pizza crust, a half-and-half combination of whole wheat and white works very well.

Whole Grains

It really is true, whole grains just have more nutrients all together. They also have more fiber than refined grains and therefore help us to feel satisfied sooner. For details on how to cook perfect brown rice and quinoa, as well as varieties of white rice, see pages 90–93.

Whole Wheat Pasta

Pasta is traditionally made with refined flour, but the addition of whole wheat options is good! Whole wheat pastas cook up to a very similar texture and taste to conventional semolina/durum pastas, but with more nutrients and fiber. You can taste a slight difference, but the great thing is that the extra fiber helps make the pasta more filling, so you'll be satisfied with less. I have found that warm dishes are better suited for whole wheat pastas than cold salads. For more details about whole wheat pasta, see page 92. ★

Pre-Soak BEANS

Most dried beans require a pre-soaking and pre-cooking process. All of the beans that are available canned (and pre-cooked) are also available dry. To use such dry beans in recipes later in this book you'll need to soak and pre-cook them before following the recipes.

∞ **Step 1:** Clean the beans.

Sort, then rinse beans with water. There may be pebbles or dirt in the beans. You want to remove those things.

∞ **Step 2:** Soak the beans. There are two options:

Long-soaking: Put a 4:1 ratio of tepid/lukewarm water to beans in a large pot and cover. Leave them to soak 6–9 hours.

Quick-soaking: Use the same ratio, but bring the water to a boil first, remove it from heat, and add the beans. Set aside, covered, for 1–2 hours.

∞ **Step 3:** Pre-cook the beans (simmer).

After soaking, strain out the soak water, rinse the beans with tepid water, and then place them in a pot with enough water to cover them. Bring to a gentle simmer, and *do not* add salt. Pre-cooking time will vary by the size of the beans and how old they are. Because of this variability, cooking progress should be checked after 45 minutes, and then again every 15–30 minutes. The beans will be ready when they are soft, smush between your fingers evenly, yet remain firm and are not falling apart.

☆ Pre-cooking time for common pre-soak beans ☆
Check after 45 minutes, then every 15–20 min.

Adzuki Beans	Black Turtle Beans
Navy Beans	Tepary Beans
Great Northern Beans	Red Kidney Beans
Cannellini (White Kidney) Beans	Black Eyed Peas
Pinto Beans	Chickpeas (Garbanzo Beans)
Pink Beans	

Once pre-cooked, these beans can be used as described in the recipes, though you may want to carefully add some salt. ½ cup dry beans yields 1½ cups cooked beans which is equal to one 15 oz can.

No-Soak BEANS

A few types of beans cook quickly and do not require extensive soaking or preparation. There's no reason to buy these pre-cooked or canned, and they aren't readily available that way anyway.

Before cooking, sort and rinse the beans to check for dirt or small pebbles. Proceed with cooking along with seasonings and vegetables as described in recipes.

☆ Standard total cooking times for no-soak beans ☆

Red Lentils	8–20 min.
Brown, Green, and French Lentils	30 min–1 hour
Yellow and Green Split Peas	45 min–1 hour
Mung Beans	1 hour

Basic Whole GRAINS

Whole grains have a happy partnership with beans and vegetables. To make sure they make *you* happy, be sure to cook them in the best way! The following can be tricky, so here are instructions for the best results:

Brown Rice

For perfect brown rice, the boiling method is easier and more reliable than the better-known simmering method.

〰 **Step 1:** Measure the rice into a bowl, add water, and swirl it around. Pour off any floating debris, then strain and rinse the rice in a fine mesh colander.

〰 **Step 2:** Bring a large pot of water to a full boil (use at least a 4:1 ratio of water to grain). Add the rice and stir. Reduce the heat to medium-high and partially cover, maintaining a boil. Boil for 30 minutes. Turn off the heat, strain the rice through the colander, and then return it to the cooking pot, covered, for 10 minutes, to steam.

Wild Rice

Wild rices are expensive, but blends of brown rices and wild rices are more affordable. I find that the best way to cook both is by the simmer method with vegetable stock or a vegetable bouillon cube.

〰 100% Wild Rice: In a pot, combine 1 part rice to 3½ parts stock or water and ½ or 1 bouillon cube. Bring to a boil, reduce to low-heat to simmer, and cover. Cook for about 45 minutes. Don't worry if there's some liquid remaining, as the vegetable broth has a nice flavor.

\\\\\ Wild Rice Blends: Use a ratio of 1 part rice to 2 parts water, and otherwise cook in the same manner as you would the 100% wild rice.

Quinoa

This little grain must be rinsed well to remove a bitter residue called saponin. It's also best when it's toasted. Then, it cooks up quickly!

\\\\\ **Step 1:** Rinse. Measure the quinoa into a bowl. Add water and swirl around with your fingers or a spoon. Pour off most of the water, and then strain the quinoa through a fine mesh strainer. Some grains will probably fall through (that's OK). While in the strainer, rinse thoroughly with tap water.

\\\\\ **Step 2:** Toast the grain. Heat a cast iron or non-stick skillet to medium heat. Transfer the wet quinoa to the skillet and allow it to heat up. Stir the grains frequently until the water has evaporated and some grains start to pop and jump.

\\\\\ **Step 3:** Cook. Add the quinoa to a pot in a 1 part quinoa to 2 parts water ratio (vegetable stock or added bouillon also works nicely). Stir and then bring the pot up to a boil, reduce the heat to low, cover, and simmer for about 15 minutes. Once done, fluff with a fork.

Millet

I haven't included recipes with millet, but it is a nutritious grain and can be used with beans and vegetables in place of rice. I like it best paired with beans that have sauces or gravies. Cooked, millet texture is fluffy and looks like half-sized, burst rice grains, and slightly resembles TVP.

〰 **Step 1**: Rinse. Measure into a bowl and add water. Swirl around with your fingers or a spoon. Pour off most of the water, and then strain the millet a fine mesh strainer. Rinse with tap water.

〰 **Step 2**: Dry and toast the grain. Heat a cast iron or non-stick skillet to medium-high heat. Transfer the wet millet to the skillet and allow it to heat up. Stir the grains frequently until the water has evaporated, slight browning occurs, and some grains start to pop and jump.

〰 **Step 3**: Cook. Bring 2 cups of water to a boil (for every 1 cup of millet). Add the millet, turn the heat to low, cover, and allow to simmer for about 15 minutes.

〰 **Step 4**: Steam. Remove from heat but leave covered for another 20 minutes.

Whole Wheat Pastas

In many dishes, whole wheat pasta can be used in place of traditional pasta. It helps to cook WWP for a minute or two longer than the same type made from refined wheat. For the typical pasta boil method, see next page.

〰 Whole wheat couscous is a pasta, too, but it is best cooked by a steam/simmer method. Use a 1:1¼ couscous to water ratio. Bring the water to a boil, remove it from the heat, add the couscous, stir, and let sit, covered, for 5–10 minutes. Fluff with a fork.

Refined GRAINS

"White" grains also love the beans and veggies. They're not as nutritious, but we all still eat them, so to make them . . .

White Rice

The simmer/steam method works well.

〰 **Step 1:** In a pot on the stovetop, combine rice, water, and a few shakes of salt. Set heat to high, watching closely until the start of a low boil.

〰 **Step 2:** Reduce heat to low, cover, and monitor for boil-over. Once the simmer has stabilized, allow to cook, covered, for 15–20 minutes. Turn off heat and let sit for 5–10 minutes.

☆ Rice types and their rice to water ratios ☆	
Basmati and Long-Grain White Rice	1:1¾
Jasmine and Medium Grain White Rice	1:1½
Pearl, Sushi, and Short-Grain White Rice	1:1¼

Refined Wheat Pastas

For perfect pasta, the boil method is most commonly used.

〰 **Step 1:** Bring ample salted water to a boil on high heat.

〰 **Step 2:** Add pasta, stir, lower heat, and partially cover with lid. Maintain a low boil, but watch for boil-over, cooking for 6–12 minutes. It is best to follow the cooking time suggested on packages. Check pasta before finishing up.

〰 **Step 3:** Strain and rinse. Toss with oil (optional).

Couscous pasta is cooked differently—see previous page.

ESSENTIAL EQUIPMENT

Every kitchen needs a basic set of mixing bowls, measuring spoons and cups, baking sheets, baking pans, and a stock pot, etc., but there are a few special items that I've found make vegan cooking and baking a lot easier.

Cast Iron Skillet

My mom still uses her grandmother's set, though I went through numerous ruined non-stick pans before I saw the light and made the switch. If seasoned well, cast iron pans will be naturally non-sticking. A 10-inch pan is great for most uses. A 12-inch pan is necessary for big jobs. Buy your pans from Lodge Cast Iron and you'll be buying Made in the USA!

Silicone Pot Handle Cover

A great invention and perfect for your cast iron handles.

Bulk Spice Jars

Spices are a big part of vegan cooking, and pre-packaged spices are usually a rip-off. You'll save a fortune by buying bulk, so either refill old spice jars (I have a few pretty, antique Spice Island jars, for example) or get yourself a jar set. Why pay $1.50 for 2 ounces of a spice you can get for $0.30 in bulk?

Air-tight Containers for Beans, Grains & Flours

Keep a stockpile of dry lentils, whole wheat pastry flour, brown rice, etc. Air-tight containers will help these to keep longer, and they'll keep out pantry pests like flour moths and flour beetles that can easily chew through plastic bags.

Cheap Coffee/Spice Grinder

Spend an extra $10 and get a coffee grinder just for flax-seeds and nuts. It's best to grind flaxseeds right before use rather than buy them pre-ground. They lose nutritional value after grinding. Flaxseeds are a great egg replacer for spice cakes and breakfast breads, and thoroughly cleaning coffee grounds out of your grinder to grind them is, well, a real pain in the ass!

Mini Whisk

You might think it's just a tchotchke from the specialty cooking store, but no! The mini whisk is indispensable for whisking egg replacer with water. I use mine all the time. It's just a bonus that it's cute.

Extra 2 Tbs Ice Cube Tray

It's very handy to have some vegetable broth cubes saved in the freezer for occasions where only a small amount of broth is needed.

I suggest an extra large-cube tray because switching between broth and water for ice might affect flavor.

Fine Mesh Strainer/Colander

A large-hole colander just won't do when you're rinsing grains like quinoa and millet. They're tiny! You must rinse quinoa, so you really do need one of these.

Wooden Stir-Fry Spatula

The wide-ended flat spatula is great for stir frying and stirring while sautéing, but also very useful when pre-toasting quinoa and millet, which requires stirring tiny grains.

Potato Masher

I didn't have one of these until a couple of years ago. What was I thinking!? It's hard to believe I managed without it. This handy tool is great for mashing potatoes, but also for mashing lentils, tofu, and bananas.

Glass Storage Containers for Leftovers and Lunches

Plastic containers aren't a good choice for reheating food in the microwave, though they're fine for cold storage. There are several nice options for glass containers in various

sizes from Pyrex, Bormioli Rocco, and others. You'll have peace of mind at lunchtime! ★

Recipe References

I dearly hope you love the recipes, coming up next! I do, and I use them often!

A few of the staple vegan recipes included here have very basic ingredients and are so consistently likeable that they appear similarly in multiple sources. I think some recipes are simple and perfect, and everyone should know them. Why fix what's not broken?

Some recipes are adapted from others in books, but with changes that I think make them better. Sometimes a small alteration makes a big difference. I've also picked up recipes from friends over the years. I love getting ideas this way, pre-tested! I mustn't forget to mention my favorite sweet treats from my mom's tattered recipe cards! I've had to "veganize" most of her baked goods, but no big deal.

Often I've developed recipes inspired by my favorite restaurant dishes, and subsequent experiments at home. Portland, Oregon, especially, is an exciting place to be vegan, and eat out! Vegetarian and vegan menu items are common, and there are a whole bunch of vegetarian restaurants and bakeries! It's all very inspiring . . . and tasty.

Reading 20 different versions of the same dish online is a fun way to research typical ingredients and variations, and for honing in on the flavor combinations I like best. The internet can be overwhelming, though, if you're not looking for something specific. Luckily, there's an ever-growing selection of great vegan cookbooks available to guide us toward foods we will love. It's absolutely delightful that the number of vegetarian and vegan cookbooks has grown so much in the past decade!

I came of age and first learned to cook in the 1990s, and many of my favorite cookbooks came out at that time are they're still in print. If you like the recipes here in *Rabbit Food Cookbook*, you may also like trying recipes from books that have inspired me and influenced my kitchen:

The American Vegetarian Cookbook from the Fit For Life Kitchen © 1990, Marilyn Diamond (A classic, large volume with health-foody, low-sugar recipes, plus lots of reference material.)

Amazing Grains: Creating Vegetarian Main Dishes with Whole Grains © 1990 Joanne Saltzman (Full of great information!)

Simply Vegan: Quick Vegetarian Meals © 1991, Barbara Wasserman and Reed Mangels PhD, RD. (Like it says, simple recipes, plus nutrition info.)

The Versatile Grain and the Elegant Bean © 1992 Sheryl and Mel London (Not exclusively vegetarian, but a great resource on beans and grains.)

The Compassionate Cook © 1993, PETA and Ingrid Newkirk (Simple and essential—my first vegan cookbook that I still use often!)

The Vegetarian No-Cholesterol Family-Style Cookbook © 1995 Kate Schumann and Virginia Messina (A great little book.)

366 Healthful Ways to Cook Tofu and other Meat Alternatives © 1996 Robin Robertson (Lots of recipes for inspiration.)

Cooking with PETA (1997) Ed. People for the Ethical Treatment of Animals (Another great collection from PETA.)

The New Farm Cookbook (1998) Ed. Louise Hagler and Dorothy Bates (A back-to-the-land '70s classic.)

Instead of Chicken, Instead of Turkey © 1999 Karen Davis (Another little gem.)

Vegan Cupcakes Take Over the World © 2006 Isa Chandra Moskowitz and Terry Hope Romero (A more recent book with a great variety of vegan cake, frosting, and glaze recipes.)

allrecipes.com, food.com, vegweb.com OK, not books, but really nice websites with many vegetarian and vegan recipes—easy to navigate online resources. ★

Measurements

for partial recipes

- USEFUL CONVERSIONS -

I gallon = 4 quarts = 3.8 liters

I quart = 2 pints = 4 cups

I pint = 2 cups

I cup = 8 fluid ounces = I6 tablespoons

$\frac{1}{3}$ cup = 5 tablespoons + I teaspoon

2 tablespoons = I ounce = $\frac{1}{8}$ cup

I tablespoon = 3 teaspoons

☆

I block tofu = (roughly) I Lb = I6 oz

I5 oz can of beans = I$\frac{1}{2}$ cup cooked beans

and $\frac{1}{2}$ to $\frac{2}{3}$ cups liquid

I tsp salt = 2360 mg sodium (U.S. RDA)

I salted vegetable bouillon cube
= I800—2200 mg sodium

When you're feeling fancier
than toast or a bowl of
cereal, or whatever it is
you usually make in the
morning... or you want
an excuse to spoil your
friends or fam' with a
brunch party...

Then again, no one would
object to the policy of
"breakfast served
all-day."

Breakfast

WAFFLES

Makes 4-5 large
waffles

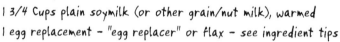

1 1/2 Cups flour

2 tsp baking powder

1/8 tsp salt

2 Tbs sugar

1 3/4 Cups plain soymilk (or other grain/nut milk), warmed

1 egg replacement - "egg replacer" or flax - see ingredient tips

2 Tbs melted vegan margarine

1 tsp vegetable oil (optional)

1/2 tsp lemon juice

pinch of cinnamon

chopped walnuts (optional)

START PREHEAT-
ING THE WAFFLE
IRON BEFORE YOU
GET STARTED.

DIRECTIONS:

In a mixing bowl, whisk together the flour, baking powder, sugar, and salt. In a separate bowl, combine warmed soymilk, oil, and melted margarine. Make one "egg" using Ener-G egg replacer or by grinding 1 Tbs flax seeds in a spice/coffee grinder & blending this with 3 Tbs tepid water in a blender. Either will work, but the flax will add extra nutrients and will have a nuttier taste. Mix wet ingredients into dry and whisk together. The batter should be pourable. Allow to rest while the waffle iron heats up. Spray some oil on the waffle iron, pour on waffles, and cook for about 6 minutes each.

EASY VEGAN PANCAKES

1 Cup all purpose or whole wheat pastry flour

1 1/2 Tbs sugar

2 tsp baking powder

1 tsp cornstarch or arrowroot

1/8 tsp salt

1 Cup soy or rice milk

2 tsp vegetable oil

1-2 tsp vegan margarine

Makes 4 large pancakes

Optional: dash of cocoa powder and cinnamon. Also try adding blueberries, chocolate chips, or chopped walnuts.

-> In a medium bowl, whisk the dry ingredients together. Next, add the oil and milk. Mix with a spoon or whisk until smooth. If batter is too thick, add a little more milk. The batter should be just thin enough to easily pour. Allow the batter to rest for a few minutes while the skillet heats up.

Brush a skillet with about 1/2 tsp margarine and heat it to medium. Pour out about 1/2 cup of the batter for each pancake to make 4 large pancakes total. Flip when the edges dull and bubble. On side 2, stab the center if you're unsure whether the middle is cooked-through.

YELLOW Scrambled TOFU

2 lbs (blocks) Firm tofu (or substitute 1/2 lb with silken)
1 medium tomato, diced
4 cloves fresh garlic, minced
1/2 onion, diced
1/2 green bell pepper, diced
1/2 red bell pepper, diced
1 Tbs vegetable oil

> OPTIONAL variation: mix 1/2 t cornstarch with 2 Tbs water, wisk, and add to tofu after 10 minutes of sautéeing.

SPICES: → → → →
*lots of turmeric   *paprika   *poultry seasoning
*black pepper   *celery seed   *salt or Bragg's aminos
*garlic powder   *dry basil

DIRECTIONS → → → → →

After adding oil, crumble the tofu with your fingers into a skillet heated to medium heat. Add a few dashes of spices, to taste, adding enough turmeric to make all the tofu yellow (2 tsp?). Stir tofu, then add all of the vegetables. Sauté for 10 minutes adding some water (about 1/4 Cup) to maintain moisture. Allow the tofu to simmer until the veggies are soft and the liquid reduces somewhat. Then eat ☺

eggless french toast

6 slices of thick, crusty bread
    - much better than regular sliced bread
1 Cup plain soymilk
2 Tbs wheat flour
2 Tbs soy flour
1 Tbs nutritional yeast
1 tsp cornstarch or arrowroot

> HINT: the toast fries up
> a bit better in margarine
> than in oil in the skillet.

1 tsp sugar
1/2 tsp vanilla
1/2 tsp cinnamon   optional-but definitely yummy:
pinch of nutmeg   2 tsp fresh orange zest
1/4 tsp salt
1/2 tsp margarine for each slice - for frying in skillet

In a mixing bowl, whisk together all INGREDIENTS...
    except for the bread & margarine
Heat a skillet to medium on the stovetop. Coat bread with the
batter mixture just before frying for about 5 minutes per side,
using about a half tsp of melted margarine for each slice.
Keep the finished slices warm in the oven, then serve hot with
powdered sugar, syrup, and orange slices or local organic
strawberries when they're in season.

MUFFINS
of many kinds

Make a basic muffin mixture first:

IN A LARGE BOWL, MIX ->

> 3 3/4 Cups flour
>   (whole wheat pastry or
>   all-purpose white)
> 1 Cup sugar
> 1 1/2 Tbs baking powder

IN A SMALL BOWL, MIX ->

> 1/2 Cup melted margarine
> 1 3/4 Cups soymilk or
>   other grain/nutmilk
> 1/2 tsp vanilla extract

FIRST: decide which flavor you're making and prep those
ingredients. See the extra ingredients over there.
THEN: preheat oven to 400°F
and set up 12-18 baking cups in muffin tins (makes 12-18 muffins).
Mix the above separately and then make a low area in the
middle of the flour mixture. Pour in the wet mixture and fold
the ingredients together gently.
   ☆ DO NOT OVER-MIX! That will make tough muffins! ☆
Fold in additional ingredients carefully. Transfer to tins and

BAKE for 20-25 minutes @ 400°F!

Choose a flavor to add:

blueberry muffins

Fold into muffin mix 1- 1 1/2 Cups frozen or fresh blueberries.

strawberry almond muffins

Fold into muffin mixture, gently, 1 1/2 Cups frozen or fresh chopped strawberries & 1/4 to 1/2 Cup sliced almonds.

lemon poppyseed muffins

Fold in: 1 Tbs lemon juice and 1 tsp vanilla + 2 tsp poppyseeds

apple cinnamon muffins

Fold in 1 to 1 1/2 Cups finely chopped apples + 1 tsp cinnamon

chocolate chip muffins

Fold in 1 cup (vegan) semi-sweet chocolate chips & 1 tsp vanilla.

Cinnamon Rolls

STEP 1
1 Tbs active dry yeast
1/2 Cup lukewarm water
1 tsp maple syrup

STEP 2 COMBINE:
3/4 Cup lukewarm water
1 Tbs maple syrup
1 Tbs melted margarine
3 Cups flour

Mix Step 1 and Step 2 SEPARATELY. When ready, add 1 to 2.

STEP 3: KNEAD dough on floured countertop for 5-7
   minutes, adding flour as needed to reduce stickiness.

STEP 4: PLACE dough in an oiled bowl and let rise 30 min.
   Then, punch this down & allow it to rise back up.

STEP 5: CUT dough into TWO pieces. Roll each half into
   a rectangle approximately 12x6 inches and between
   1/4 and 1/2 inch thick.

STEP 6: PREHEAT OVEN TO 375°F

STEP 7: Prepare sweet gooey part:
   6 Tbs vegan margarine
   2 tsp cinnamon
   1 Cup brown sugar
   1/2 Cup chopped pecans

BRUSH the margarine
onto dough and then
generously drizzle
other ingredients on top,
leaving some extra.

STEP 8: ROLL dough and cut each piece into 6 equal rolls.

STEP 9: PLACE some extra gooey mix in the bottom of a 12x9"
   pan. Place rolls in pan, let them rise for 30 minutes and
   then bake for 15 min. at 375°.

STEP 10: Flip over baked rolls and
   drizzle on icing composed of
1/2 Cup powdered sugar + 1 Tbs
lemon juice, mixed until smooth. YUM!

crumbly coffee cake

3 Cups flour
3/4 Cup sugar
1/4 Cup brown sugar
3/4 Cup cold vegan margarine, in bits

for STRAWBERRY ALMOND   -or-
1/2 tsp cinnamon
1/4 tsp nutmeg
1/4 tsp allspice

for APPLE WALNUT
1 1/2 tsp cinnamon
1/2 tsp nutmeg
1/2 tsp allspice

Mix flour, sugars, & spices. Cut in margarine and mix thoroughly by smushing between fingers until struesel texture forms.
*Set aside 1 Cup of this to use in the crumbly topping.

1 1/3 Cups plain soymilk or almond milk
3 Tbs baking powder
1 1/2 Cups chopped fruit - strawberries / apple / other
1/2 Cup chopped nuts - (slivered) almonds / walnuts

2 Tbs brown sugar

After 1 Cup is removed, add baking powder, soymilk, fruit, and half of the nuts to form the batter. Mix gently - don't over-mix! Pour into a greased and floured 8 x 8 inch baking pan.

FOR TOPPING: Mix 2 Tbs brown sugar and remainder of nuts into the 1 cup of struesel topping you set aside earlier, and then sprinkle that on top of the batter before baking.

Bake for 30 minutes at 375°F.

☆EASY☆
BAKING POWDER
BISCUITS

2 Cups flour (or so)

1 Tbs baking powder

1/2 tsp salt

1/4 Cup (cold) vegan margarine
(or sub. shortening)

1 Cup plain soymilk

PREHEAT OVEN to 450° F

1. Whisk together flour, baking soda, and salt.

2. Cut cold margarine into small slices and add to flour mix, coating well. Then, use your fingers to smush the flour and margarine together (for about 5 minutes) until the mixture resembles a fine, crumbly streusel.

3. Add soymilk and stir just until liquid is taken up. Add a little more flour if dough is too sticky to knead.

4. Gather together dough, then knead & fold it on a floured surface 10 times, not more. While kneading, add flour to de-sticky it more, if necessary.

5. Spread dough into a 1/2 inch thick round & cut out biscuits with the mouth of a glass.

6. Place on a greased baking sheet and bake 'em for 12-15 minutes.

* makes about 14 small biscuits *

Almond GRAVY

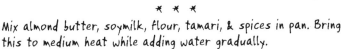

1/2 Cup unsalted almond butter
1/2 Cup plain soymilk
4 Tbs flour
2 tsp low-sodium tamari
2 1/4 tsp onion powder
3/4 tsp garlic powder
pinch of poultry seasoning & black pepper
1 1/2 Cups (or so) water
1/2 to 3/4 tsp salt (or, to taste)

* * *

Mix almond butter, soymilk, flour, tamari, & spices in pan. Bring this to medium heat while adding water gradually.

Stir at a simmer for about 10 minutes. Add salt (or additional tamari or Bragg Aminos) to taste. Voila! Add more water later if you reheat the gravy.

Serve over biscuits — or other things like potatoes, breaded tofu/tempeh in place of brown gravy.
mmm... but, use some restraint —> this gravy goop is rich!

Fruity Raisin Bran Muffins

1 Cup orange juice
1/2 Cup rice milk
1/4 Cup canola oil
2 Ener-G or Flaxseed egg replacements (see ingredient tips)
1/4 tsp vanilla extract
1/2 Cup brown sugar   1/4 Cup raisins
2 1/2 Cups raisin bran cereal   1 Cup dried date pieces
1/4 Cup chopped walnuts (opt)

- -

1 1/2 Cups + 2 Tbs whole wheat pastry flour
2 tsp baking powder
1/2 tsp baking soda

In a large mixing bowl, combine orange juice, rice milk, oil, egg substitutes, vanilla, and brown sugar. Mix well. Add the cereal, dates, and extra raisins.
Now: Preheat the oven to 400°F. Prep muffin tins & baking cups. This will divide well into 18 standard muffins, so plan accordingly.
In a separate bowl, combine the flour, baking soda, and baking powder. Whisk together well. Add this to the wet mixture, stir gently until well mixed and a bit creamed looking. Quickly, move on to filling the baking cups evenly, and then bake for about 17 minutes.

A fabulous way to eat
something healthful for
days and days on end, an
excellent excuse to shop
for or bake fresh bread,
and an easy way to feed a
whole bunch of folks...

(Okay, so don't overlook the
part about the bread. It's
important.)

Soups

Black Bean Soup

4 Cans (15oz) low-salt black beans
    with the liquid <or>
    strained & rinsed with 2 more cups of water added
1 Cup water
1 medium red onion, chopped (or 1/2 large onion)
3-4 celery ribs
4 cloves garlic, minced
1/2 red bell pepper, diced
1 small tomato, diced
1 bay leaf (remove after cooking-not edible)
1/2 tsp black pepper
1/2 tsp chili powder
1/4 tsp sage powder
2 dashes of hot sauce (optional)

CUT UP VEGETABLES nice and small. Heat a large pot to medium-low heat. Add black beans from cans, with the liquid, or rinse and add extra water as specified above. Add everything else, stir, and let simmer for about 30-40 minutes to let the veggies soften and the flavor soak into the broth. It's ready when the celery is soft.
Add one cup pre-cooked rice when soup is done, if desired.

 SERVE HOT

☆ TOFU-VEGETABLE SOUP ☆

10 cups of water

VEGETABLES:

2-3 large potatoes, cut up

1 lb firm tofu, cubed up small

2-3 Cups chopped celery

2 small tomatoes, chopped

1 white or yellow onion, chopped

2 Cups fresh or frozen green beans

2 tsp vegetable oil

5-6 cloves fresh garlic, minced

1 small carrot, chopped

1/2 to 1 cup tomato sauce (or left-over marinara or pizza sauce)

SPICES:

1 vegetarian no-salt vegetable bouillon cube

1 Tbs basil   2 tsp pepper or lemon pepper

1/2 tsp paprika   salt, to taste

1/4 tsp savory   1-2 tsp garlic powder

1 tsp celery seed

START a large stock pot on medium heat with 10 cups of water. Chop vegetables. Add the bouillon cube, then potatoes, other veggies, sauce, and spices. Adjust the salt and other spices to your taste. Lower the heat to a simmer, cover and cook for about an hour until potatoes and celery are soft and the broth is robust.

This is my very favorite soup!

119

LENTIL SOUP

4 Cups dry lentils
about 12 Cups water
1 (unsalted) vegetable
    bouillon cube
1 medium onion, diced
2 medium potatoes, cubed
4 celery ribs, diced
2 medium tomatoes, diced
1 red bell pepper, diced
1 carrot, chopped small
2 Tbs Bragg Aminos (optional)
2 Tbs vegetable oil
2 tsp black pepper
1 Tbs curry powder
1/2 tsp chili powder
salt (adjust to taste)

Cut up vegetables. Put water in a large pot and add the bouillon cube and lentils. Bring this to medium heat. Add veggies, spices, and oil. Turn down the heat to a simmer to cook for about 1 hour total, or until lentils are soft but not falling apart. Remove from heat and make a final adjustment to the salt and spices, to taste.

SPLIT PEA & POTATO SOUP

about 7 Cups of water
3 large potatoes - or several smaller potatoes
1 medium onion, diced
4 garlic cloves, minced
2 Cups chopped celery, including leaves/tops
1 1/2 Cups plain soymilk
2 Cups yellow split peas, rinsed

SPICES:
1 unsalted vegetable bouillon cube (optional)
Lots of dry basil (about 2 Tbs?)
lemon pepper or black pepper
salt - to taste
garlic powder
celery seed
tarragon

BEGIN COOKING the split peas in the water first.
Cook them on medium heat for about half an hour before adding the potatoes, spices, soymilk, and other vegetables. Cook
everything together on a simmer for about another half an hour.
Add the spices to your preference, a few dashes at a time.
WHEN DONE, the split peas should be soft but not completely
mushy. Do last minute spicing and seasoning to taste. Allow to
cool slightly and then remove some of the soup to PUREE it in a
blender, to enhance the creamy texture of the finished soup.

Potato-Leek Soup

1 large leek, washed and chopped up
3 medium to large potatoes, cubed
4 cloves garlic, minced
5 or more of those funny garlic spears, -->
    chopped (seasonal, in summer)
2 tsp olive oil
1-2 tsp salt (to taste)
1 tsp black pepper
1/2 tsp onion powder
1 Cup plain soymilk
6 1/2 Cups water

① Sauté leeks & garlic in some oil for 10 minutes
    in the bottom of a stock pot.

② Add water, allow it to heat up, and then simmer the potatoes, leeks, & garlic spears (cut into little round segments) with
spices & oil for about an hour. When the soup is almost done,
add the soymilk and salt, to taste. Cook until the potatoes are
smushy.

basic
MISO SOUP
FOR TWO

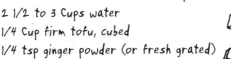

1 tsp vegetable oil
2 Tbs diced white onion
2 Tbs slivered shiitake mushrooms,
     sautéed in oil (optional)
2 1/2 to 3 Cups water
1/4 Cup firm tofu, cubed
1/4 tsp ginger powder (or fresh grated)
1 clove garlic, minced
1/4 Cup other veggies — i.e. julienned carrot, sliced
     celery, snow peas, broccoli, etc. (optional)
1/4 Cup green onions, chopped
1 1/2 Tbs mellow white miso soybean paste
a dash of pepper & a dash of tamari

IN A MEDIUM POT, heat oil on medium.
Add white onion & mushrooms and sauté until they are
 both sort of brown/caramelized.
Add water, spices, garlic, & tofu and bring to a simmer.
Add other vegetables and cook for 5 minutes.
Add miso paste, stirring well to break it apart.

Lastly, add green onion, simmer just a couple minutes more and
then serve! For the simplest soup don't include "other veggies."

Spicy *slimming* Cabbage Soup

also known as
Oh dear I've been
eating out too much
lately Soup.

14 Cups water
1 medium leek – chopped
4 large garlic cloves, minced
1/2 jalapeño pepper, carefully minced
      (use more if you're so inclined)
1 1/2 large carrots, julienned into
      cute little sticks
2 medium red potatoes
      sliced and also cut into little sticks   like this
4 large celery ribs, chopped
1 medium tomato, diced small
1 no-salt or low salt vegetable bouillon cube
1 cup spicy tomato-vegetable juice
SPICES:
2-3 tsp powdered mustard   black pepper – to taste
2 tsp coriander   lemon pepper (a few dashes)
1 bay leaf   salt – add to taste
Dashes of basil, thyme, and rosemary
AND FINALLY,
1/2 head Napa cabbage, chopped/shredded
1/2 head green cabbage, chopped/shredded (keep these separate)
      (or use 1 whole of either)   Now, for the instructions...

Spicy Cabbage Soup instructions

* Fill a large stock pot with 14-16 cups of water. Add the bouillon cube and heat to medium.

* In a 10 inch or so skillet, sauté in about a teaspoon of vegetable oil, the onion, leek, jalapeño, garlic, and celery until they soften somewhat.

* Cut the carrots and potatoes just like I said over there, no cheating, and then add them and the diced tomato to the pot.

* Add the spices, vegetable juice, and the sautéed vegetables to the pot. Do not add the cabbage yet! Hold your horses!

* Simmer everything (except for the cabbage) until the celery is no longer crunchy. This might take about 30-40 minutes.

* Once everything else is softened, finally you can add the cabbage. If you use two kinds of cabbage, add the green cabbage first, allow to simmer for about 3 minutes, and then add the napa cabbage. Otherwise, allow the napa cabbage to simmer for about 5 minutes, maximum, and the green cabbage, about 8 minutes tops.

** Remove from the heat, adjust salt level to your taste, and eat as much as you want (instead of eating tortilla chips and cookies which is why you probably decided it was time to make cabbage soup in the first place ☺). **

HEARTY BLACK-EYED PEA

6 Cups water
1 bay leaf
1/2 or 1 vegetarian bouillon cube
3 (15oz) cans black eyed peas, strained
1 Cup diced white or yellow onion (approximately 1 medium)
3/4 Cup diced celery
1 medium tomato, diced
2 cloves garlic, minced

1/2 tsp black pepper
1/4 tsp liquid smoke
a couple of dashes of turmeric & celery seed
1/4 tsp Emril's Essence or other Cajun seasoning
1/4 tsp vegetarian bacon seasoning (optional)
(I use Bakon brand hickory smoke style dried yeast seasoning)

pinch of paprika & of cumin
2 tsp olive oil

---

2 vegetarian kielbasa or veggie Italian sausages, cut into small
    pieces and sautéed in olive oil (I use Tofurky brand)

DIRECTIONS: Strain and rinse the beans to reduce sodium.
Preserve 1 cup of liquid from the cans and substitute it for 1
cup of water if you're not too concerned about salt. In a soup
pot, heat water with bouillon on medium heat. Add the beans and
bring to a simmer. Add the bay leaf and vegetables, and then
the spices & oil. In a skillet, sauté the pieces of veggie sausage
in olive oil until browned on both sides, and then add to soup.
Simmer for about 15 more minutes, or until celery is soft.
Add cayenne pepper also, to taste, if you're the hot and peppery
type.

Yes, but remember how we talked about "varied and healthful":

a. Whether or not it's true, let's assume you already know how to make a lovely green salad, boil edamame or fresh green beans, and slice up fruit.

b. However tempting, it is not recommended to restrict your diet to tofu pot pie entirely.

Main Meals

BREADED TOFU

1/3 Cup nutritional yeast flakes
1/4 Cup flour
1/2 tsp garlic powder
1/2 tsp salt
1/2 tsp black pepper
1/2 tsp poultry seasoning
1/2 tsp cayenne pepper (optional)

1 lb (block/cake) Firm tofu, cut into small 1/2 inch cubes
1-2 Tbs vegetable oil

MIX everything (except for the tofu & oil) in a paper or plastic
bag. Squeeze out some of the water in the tofu and cube it
up before putting it in the bag. Shake well and get all the tofu
covered.
Heat the vegetable oil in a large skillet on med-high heat, adding
the covered tofu once it's hot. For best results, use a pan large
enough for the tofu cubes to not be crowded. Sauté and stir
frequently until tofu breading is browned.
This is good alone as a snack, or as finger food with BBQ
sauce, or honey-mustard sauce. You can also use this recipe
to add breading to slabs of tofu for sandwiches or use the
cubes (like chicken is sometimes used) on a deluxe salad! mmm!

Alternate
BREADING
For Tofu, Tempeh, or Seitan

In a medium bowl, mix together:

1/3 Cup unbleached flour

1/4 Cup nutritional yeast flakes

1/4 Cup cornmeal

1/4 tsp paprika (milder)
    or cayenne pepper (hotter)

1 tsp garlic powder	1 tsp salt
1 tsp poultry seasoning	1 tsp black pepper
1/2 tsp onion powder	1 tsp cornstarch

2 Tbs vegetable oil

1-1.5 lbs tofu, (steamed) tempeh, or seitan, in bite sized pieces

DIRECTIONS ⟹

Mix breading ingredients well.
Place (drained) seitan, (steamed) tempeh, or
(squeezed) firm tofu pieces into bowl, turning and
mixing to cover well (you may have excess breading
mix left). Heat oil in skillet to medium-high heat
and then fry pieces, stirring and turning until
they're nicely browned. Use next with sauce of
choice, in burritos, with vegetables in a stir fry,
or eat all alone!

Super Breaded Tofu "Fried Chicken"-y Dinner

1 lb breaded tofu (see recipe)
1 large carrot, julienned
1-2 Cups fresh or frozen
    green beans, cut up
1 small white or yellow onion, chopped
2 tsp vegetable oil

Don't eat me, eat tofu!

2 medium potatoes, boiled & mashed
1/4 tsp garlic powder
1/4 tsp salt, or to taste
1/4 tsp black pepper
vegetarian brown gravy or mushroom gravy, prepared

- - - - -

In a large skillet, prepare the tofu first, following the breaded tofu or alternate breading recipe. At the same time, boil the potatoes in a separate pot until soft. Once tofu is browned, add carrots, green beans, and onion. Add a bit of extra oil and stir. Cook covered, on medium-low heat, stirring often, until veggies soften. Mash the potatoes, add spices, and set aside. Make some gravy (see Brown Gravy recipe, or use an instant mix). Finally, mix mashed potatoes with tofu and veggies, or serve the tofu mix over the potatoes, with gravy. Mm, Mmmmm, Mmm!

BROWN

A bit more healthful
than a gravy mix
packet! and,
vegan.

GRAVY

1 Tbs olive oil
1 Tbs nutritional yeast
2 Tbs wheat or garbanzo flour
1/4 Cup plain soymilk or almond milk
2 Cups vegetable stock
 or 1 veg. bouillon cube dissolved in 2 Cups of water
1 tsp low-sodium tamari
2 Tbs cornstarch mixed into 2 Tbs cold water
1 tsp onion powder
1/2 tsp garlic powder
1/2 tsp poultry seasoning
1/4 to 1/2 tsp black pepper
add salt to taste - only if bouillon/stock is unsalted

OKay... First, in a pan on medium-low heat mix the oil, nutritional yeast & flour into a paste. Stir for about 5 minutes until it starts to brown. Remove from the heat and mix in soymilk, stir back into a paste, add about 1/2 cup of stock, whisk together, and place back onto heat. Next add tamari, cornstarch pre-mixed with water, and spices. Stir in the rest of the stock slowly until the gravy simmers and thickens. Have yourself a taste and then add additional salt only if necessary.

Ohio Valley TOFU

mmm...

Vegetable oil
1-2 lbs extra firm tofu, cubed
1 Cup, or a handful of fresh green
    beans, cut up
1 small/med onion, cut up
1/2 to 1 average carrot, cut up
1 medium potato, cut up
1 head fresh broccoli, cut up
1/2 green bell pepper, cut up (optional)
1/2 Cup mushrooms, cut and sautéed first separately (optional)
    <<Add other veggies that sound good to you, if desired>>
Many dashes of tamari/soy sauce and Bragg Aminos.

USE THESE SPICES:
salt & black pepper
garlic powder
chili powder
turmeric

Note: When you start cooking, also separately
start 1/2 Cup of rice, boiled in water
according to the variety, to mix in at the end.

COOK tofu in a medium-hot skillet with oil, tamari, and Bragg
Aminos until the tofu begins to look browned and shrively.
Next, add potato bits, then green beans, onion, etc. Add spices
to taste.
Turn down the heat to medium-low and cook covered, stirring
occasionally, until the potatoes are soft. When the tofu and
veggies are done, mix in rice.

Tofu Knishes

← 4" →

5"

(Fold up)

FIRST → BEGIN BY BOILING 2 1/2 CUPS POTATOES (TO MASH)

NEXT: MAKE DOUGH

1 Cup mashed potatoes
1 Tbs vegetable oil
3 Cups unbleached flour
1 tsp baking powder
1/2 Cup cold water
1 tsp salt

THEN: MAKE FILLING

1 Cup diced onion
1 lb block firm tofu, mashed
1 1/2 Cups mashed potatoes
1 Cup green peas
2 Tbs vegetable oil
1 Tbs dry parsley
        (or use fresh)
1 tsp salt
1/2 tsp garlic powder
1/4 tsp black pepper

Boil the potatoes and then mash them up once they're soft. Mix one Cup of mashed potatoes with oil & salt. Add flour, baking powder, and then water. Mix and then knead until dough is smooth. Let the dough rest for 30 minutes on a board.

☆ HEAT OVEN TO 350°F ☆

Sauté the onion in oil until softened. In a large bowl, mix together crumbled/mashed tofu, potatoes, onion, spices, and peas.
THEN...
Divide the dough into 12-16 equal pieces. Roll out each piece thinly in a rectangle, and fill with a scoop of filling. Fold dough like in the illustration above and place on baking pan, fold-down.

⁂ BAKE 25 MINUTES ⁂

Best when served with vegetarian brown gravy on top
(See brown gravy recipe, or use vegetarian instant packets).

"Meaty" Spaghetti
For Two

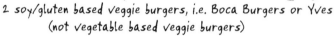

INGREDIENTS

2 of what you deem to be servings of spaghetti
    noodles — try using whole wheat!
1/2 to 3/4 of a 10 oz jar of marinara sauce
2 soy/gluten based veggie burgers, i.e. Boca Burgers or Yves
    (not vegetable based veggie burgers)
2 tsp vegetable oil (approximately)
Bragg Aminos
SPICES: (Approximate) 1/2 tsp basil, 1/4 tsp or 3 cloves fresh
garlic, minced, and black pepper, to taste.

DIRECTIONS

① Cook spaghetti. Strain, rinse, and set aside.
② Heat oil in skillet on medium. Add 2 veggie burgers and
    allow them to defrost, if frozen, turning on both sides.
③ When tender, break up burgers into small pieces using the
    spatula.
④ Add dry basil, garlic or garlic powder, pepper, and dashes
    of Bragg Aminos to taste and stir.
⑤ Stir occasionally for about 10 min. until burgers are well
    done and slightly seared (but not totally burnt).
⑥ Mix sauce with burger mixture (or also with the spaghetti
    noodles) on low heat until sauce is hot. Serve. ☆

TOFU POT PIE

INCLUDES:
PIE CRUST, FILLING,
& GRAVY.

so good!!

① JOSH'S PIE CRUST

For one pot pie - top and bottom crusts

1 3/4 Cups unbleached flour
1/2 Cup vegetable oil
1/3 Cup plain soymilk
pinch of salt

Mix everything
together; knead.
Set aside while
preparing filling
for pie. See part
4 directions.

② VEGAN NUTRITIONAL YEAST GRAVY ☆

2 Cups boiling water
2 Tbs vegetable oil
1 vegetable bouillon cube
3 Tbs nutritional yeast flakes
about 1/2 Cup unbleached flour
1/4 tsp black pepper
1/4 tsp poultry seasoning
1/2 Cup diced onion

Boil water, add the
bouillon cube and oil,
mix together flour
& yeast and then
add SLOWLY while
whisking, stirring
out lumps. Add diced
onion last. Stir and
cook on low to me-
dium heat until thick.
SET ASIDE.

③ POT PIE FILLING

START BY BREADING SOME TOFU:

1/4 Cup flour
1 Tbs nutritional yeast flakes
1 tsp salt
3/4 tsp garlic powder
1/2 tsp black pepper
1/2 tsp poultry seasoning

→ | Shake to mix everything but the tofu together in paper or plastic bag. Add tofu cubes and shake to coat well.

1 lb (block) firm tofu, cubed

IN A LARGE SKILLET WITH 2 TBS VEGETABLE OIL:

Sauté together on medium heat ->

   1 lb breaded tofu (from above)
   1 Cup chopped potato
   1 Cup chopped celery
   1/2 Cup chopped carrot
   1/2 Cup green peas
   1 Cup diced onion

Stir frequently, cooking for about
20 minutes total, or until the potatoes start to soften up. They
don't have to be completely done, as they will cook more in
the oven. Remove from heat and mix in the gravy from part 2
(previous page).

④ DIRECTIONS FOR POT PIE MAKING

* Preheat the oven to 450°F. Make the dough (Part 1) and then separate it into two slightly unequal pieces. Roll out the larger piece between two sheets of parchment paper (do this, trust me) and then lay it into the pie pan. Cover the crust with foil, fill it with dry beans or pie weights (do this too, trust me!), and bake it for 7 minutes. Remove from oven & set aside the bottom crust + the extra dough.

Decrease oven temperature to 375°F

NEXT! * Prepare the nutritional yeast gravy (Part 2) and the breaded tofu and vegetable filling (Part 3), per the instructions. These can be done at the same time, working on the gravy while the tofu and veggies cook.

THEN! * Add the gravy to the pan of tofu-vegetable filling, mixing well. Then pack it all into the pre-cooked bottom pie crust in the pie pan. Pat down the filling to remove pockets of air.

AT LAST! * Roll out the second half of the pie crust dough (between the two pieces of parchment paper). Drape and position the top crust dough over the filling, and pinch it together at the edges with the bottom crust. Using a sharp knife, cut a few decorative vents in the top.

Bake your pot pie at 375°F
for 30 minutes

You'll wish you'd made two!

SCRATCH PIZZA or breadsticks

2 tsp active dry yeast
4+ Cups whole wheat pastry flour
       or mix of unbleached white & whole wheat flours
1 1/4 Cups warm water (100°F)
3 Tbs olive oil
1/2 tsp sugar; 1/4 tsp salt
SPICES: add a dash or 2 of garlic powder, black pepper, thyme, basil, oregano, red pepper flakes.

COMBINE yeast, sugar, & 1 cup flour. Add the warm water & let sit 10 minutes. Mix in oil and spices. Then begin to add flour one cup at a time until kneading is required. Knead in 1/2 cup at a time until the dough is no longer sticky in your hands.

SEPARATE dough into 2 parts and let rise, covered, on oiled pizza pans for 30-60 min (better results when left to rise).

FOR PIZZA -> Prepare sauce and toppings while dough rises. Preheat oven to 475°F. Spread dough onto 2 pans evenly and cover with sauce and toppings. Let sit 5-10 min. Bake for 5 minutes, switch top & bottom pans, and bake 5 more minutes.

FOR BREADSTICKS -> Preheat oven to 450°F. Roll out 1/2 dough into a rectangle on a rectangular pan, & cut into 8 slices using a pastry cutter. Let stand for 15 min. Bake for about 8 minutes.

PIZZA SAUCE & TOPPING

SAUCE:

Pizza sauce can be made easily by adding a few things to a can of tomato sauce (and it will cost less than a jar of pizza sauce).

1 can tomato sauce
1/2 to 1 can tomato paste
2 tsp olive oil
2 tsp sugar
a few dashes of spices: basil, garlic powder, black pepper, oregano, thyme, rosemary, red pepper flakes (optional)

MIX TOGETHER all ingredients in a bowl and spread on pizzas. Using more tomato paste makes for a thicker sauce. Covers two 12-inch pizzas. This can also be heated on the stovetop to use with breadsticks.

TOFU "SAUSAGE" PIZZA TOPPING ⟶

For two 12" pizzas, use 1/2 to 3/4 lb of firm tofu.

Crumble tofu into skillet and sauté in vegetable oil on medium heat. Add enough tamari to make the tofu browned. Also add about 1 tsp of Bragg Aminos. Spice the crumbles with garlic, black pepper, basil, and just a drop of liquid smoke flavor seasoning. Cook, stirring occasionally, for about 10 minutes or long enough that the tofu is browned and slightly crunchy. ADD to pizza as a topping before baking. Works great as a taco filling too!

PASTA with WHITE BEANS

a new favorite!

2 cups dry small whole wheat pasta
   cooked separately in water, strained, and set aside
2 tsp to 1 Tbs olive oil
1 medium white or yellow onion, diced
3 cloves garlic, chopped
1 (15oz) can navy beans (small) or canellini beans (medium)
   - strained and rinsed well
1 (15oz) can italian-style diced tomatoes
    -or- 2 cups fresh diced tomatoes
1-2 tsp fresh rosemary, minced
a few dashes of: fresh ground pepper, dry basil, & dry oregano

---

☺ Cook your 2 cups of small whole wheat pasta (shells, macaroni, or penne for example), strain and set aside.

☺ Heat olive oil in a 10 inch skillet on medium heat. Add diced onion and sauté for about 5 min. Add garlic and sauté until the onions are softened.

☺ Next, strain and rinse the beans and add them to the pan. stir occasionally for several minutes.

☺ Add the canned or fresh tomatoes, rosemary, and other spices. Cover and allow to simmer for about 10 more minutes. If using fresh tomatoes, add salt, to taste.

☺ Turn off heat and either mix with or serve over the pasta.

☺ Variation: cut a veggie "italian sausage" (I use the Tofurky ones) into quartered rounds, sauté in olive oil until browned, and then add to the dish!

EASY lentils ★

1
→ 2 Cups dry brown/green lentils, rinsed
5 Cups water (approximately)
1 vegetable bouillon cube –required!
1/2–3/4 tsp salt (adjust to taste)

2
→ 1 larger or 2 small potatoes, diced
1/2 medium onion, diced
1 medium tomato, diced

MAKES 4 SERVINGS

3
→ 3 cloves garlic, minced   – or –   1/2 tsp garlic powder
1 tsp olive oil   1/2 tsp black pepper
1/4 tsp sage powder   1/8–1/4 tsp celery seed
1/8–1/4 tsp paprika   pinch of cayenne pepper
2 or more tsp Bragg Aminos   pinch of turmeric
                                                  pinch of marjoram

DIRECTIONS: Rinse lentils in a mesh strainer and then put them in a pot with water and bouillon cube on medium–high heat. Add the potatoes, onion, and tomato. Decrease heat to medium–low for a low simmer. Add the garlic and other spices and cover, stirring occasionally, to cook for a total of about 40 minutes. When done, the potatoes & lentils will be soft, but not totally mushy, and there should be a small amount of liquid keeping the lentils moist. SERVE WITH FRESH BAGUETTE!

COLD BLACK BEAN SALAD

Kernels from 1-2 ears of fresh corn
(or about 1 cup frozen sweet corn)
3 (15oz) cans of black beans, strained & rinsed
1 green bell pepper, diced
1 red bell pepper, diced
1 yellow bell pepper, diced
1/2 medium red onion, diced
1 small to medium tomato, diced
1 clove garlic, minced
4-5 Tbs red wine vinegar
fresh ground black pepper
2 Tbs olive oil

GOOD FOR SUMMER

☆☆☆ PUT CORN KERNELS into boiling water for two minutes, then remove from heat & strain (or defrost about 1 cup of frozen corn if it's not summer). Chop up the onion, and rinse it well in a mesh strainer to reduce some of its pungency. Chop peppers and tomato and combine all vegetables and seasonings with oil & vinegar, and mix well. FINALLY: mix in the rinsed black beans. Chill for a couple of hours, or overnight for best flavor, and serve.

*For a mellower taste, use a little bit less
of the onion and vinegar.

Savory Tofu-Potato Burritos

3-4 servings

☆ 1 lb tofu or tempeh, cut into
   1/2 inch cubes
☆ 2 medium red potatoes or 1 large russet
   cut into small pieces
☆ 1/2 medium onion, diced
☆ 1/2 green bell pepper, diced
☆ 1 medium tomato, diced
   about 1 Tbs Bragg Aminos
   vegetable oil

> SERVE →
> with Flour
> tortillas, lettuce,
> and a few
> dollops of pizza
> sauce — or
> serve with hot
> sauce or salsa

SPICES : Approximately...
1 tsp each of turmeric & garlic powder
1/4 to 1/2 tsp each of salt & black pepper —or to taste
1/4 to 1/2 tsp each of sage, basil, thyme, chili powder,
   savory, nutritional yeast flakes, paprika, & rosemary.

DIRECTIONS :

Sauté tofu and/or tempeh with potatoes, garlic & turmeric for
5 minutes on medium heat. Add other vegetables, Bragg Aminos,
& other spices, stirring occasionally for 5-10 min.
Add 1/2 cup water, lower heat, cover, & let simmer until potatoes are soft, water has reduced, and spices have soaked in.
Adjust salt to taste. Serving suggestion above.

"Kind-of Like
Chicken" fajitas

1 lb block firm tofu, cut in strips
1/2 med. onion, diced
1/2 red bell pepper, cut
1 small tomato, diced
some lettuce
burrito shells
"Nayonaise" or other vegan mayo dressing
vegetable oil

Or 'chickeny'
slab o' tofu
sandwiches

SPICES: Bragg Aminos, garlic powder, salt,
     black pepper, poultry seasoning, paprika or
     cayenne, dry basil, & nutritional yeast flakes.

(1) Cut tofu into strips and sauté in skillet on med-high
     heat, adding all seasonings in dashes, to taste.

(2) Add onion & red pepper and sauté until the onion softens.

(3) Don't forget to add plenty of Bragg Aminos.

Make wraps with this filling: spread Nayonaise on the shells;
add lettuce and fresh tomatoes, tofu and veggies.   or...

** 1 pound of firm tofu also yields five slab cutlets of tofu –
cook one or more tofu slabs with the same spices, but prepare
them in sandwiches on toasted bread instead of burrito shells.
Yum! So good! **

tex-mex tofu fajitas

(Similar to the "chicken" flavor fajitas, but with different spices and vegetables.)

* 1 lb block firm tofu, pressed - or tofu frozen & thawed. and cut into strips.

⟶ Sauté the tofu alone with oil on medium-high heat

SEASON with: garlic powder, chili powder, a dash of sugar, black pepper, salt or seasoned salt, Bragg Aminos, mustard seed, onion powder, and a dash each of cayenne and tamari.

- -

* VEGETABLES to sauté - add after tofu is coated:
Onion - green and/or red bell pepper - carrots, julienned - zucchini and/or yellow squash - fresh/frozen corn

* SERVE with the following raw vegetables:
diced tomato - avocado - shredded red cabbage and/or
lettuce

IN flour or corn tortillas
WITH hot sauce or salsa and crushed tortilla chips,

Serve with rice and black beans or pinto beans, if you want to impress everyone further with your super deluxe vegan fajitas!

SEITAN *from Scratch*

STORE-BOUGHT SEITAN CAN BE EXPENSIVE. THIS
HOME-MADE VERSION IS A BARGAIN. TAKES 1.5 HRS

PART 1

1 1/2 Cups (wheat) gluten flour   Mix these together
3 Tbs whole wheat flour
2 Tbs nutritional yeast flakes
1/2 tsp garlic powder
1/2 tsp onion granules

PART 2

Dissolve the bouillon cube in
1 1/4 Cup hot water   water. Add to part 1 and mix.
1 vegetable bouillon cube   Knead together for 5 min. on
              (unsalted)   a flat surface. Add a little
                                    more flour if the dough isn't
PART 3   firm enough.

In a large pot, combine: Combine everything in a large
10-12 Cups water   pot when the water is still
1/2 Cup tamari   cold. Cut the dough into 4
4 cloves garlic, chopped   pieces & add to the pot. Bring
1/2 onion, sliced   the water to a boil and then
1 bay leaf   turn it down to a simmer,
1/2 tsp black pepper   cooking for 1 hour.
1/2 tsp ginger powder

STORE seitan in its broth in the fridge
or freezer if not used immediately.

Things to do with Seitan

① BBQ SEITAN

1/2 Cup seitan slices
2 slices of onion, chopped
vegetable oil
BBQ sauce

Sauté seitan slices with onion (optional) in oil. Decrease heat to low and coat with your favorite barbecue sauce. Eat as is, or in a sandwich with toasted bread & lettuce.

② SEITAN WITH PEPPERS & ONIONS

2 tsp vegetable oil
1 Cup seitan slices
1/4 medium onion, sliced
1/2 red bell pepper, sliced
other veggies, or crimini mushrooms - optional
SPICES: black pepper, garlic powder, ground ginger
1 tsp arrowroot or cornstarch
1/3 to 1/2 Cup cold seitan broth or water
1 tsp flour

Sauté the seitan, vegetables, & spices in oil in a skillet for 5-10 minutes, until browned. Mix the arrowroot and flour with about 1/3 Cup COLD broth in a small bowl. When vegetables have desired tenderness, decrease heat to low, add the arrowroot mixture, and stir until thickened.
Great when served with mashed potatoes! ☆

SEITAN WALNUT basil QUINOA (OR) COUSCOUS

FOR QUINOA:
1 Cup dry red (or white) quinoa
2 Cups water
1/2 unsalted veg. bouillon cube
  -or-
FOR COUSCOUS:
1 Cup dry couscous
1 1/4 Cups water
1/2 unsalted veg. bouillon cube

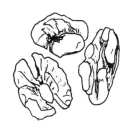

THE REST OF THE DISH:
1 Tbs olive oil
1 Cup chopped seitan (or 1 package, if you buy pre-made)
1 Cup chopped or halved walnut pieces
1/2 tsp salt
1 small red bell pepper, diced

AND THEN,
1 Tbs olive oil (yep, again)
1 Tbs lemon juice
1/2 Cup fresh basil, chopped -   do not substitute dry basil! no!
1/8 tsp black pepper

Directions for Seitan Walnut Basil Quinoa or Couscous

LET'S GET STARTED!

---------- QUINOA -----------

※ If you're making quinoa, place it in a bowl with water, stir it around, and then slowly pour the water and the quinoa through a fine mesh strainer. Rinse more in the strainer, and then place the quinoa in a skillet on med. heat. Stir until it's a little browned and dry again.

※ Place water, prepped quinoa, & bouillon in a pan, break up the bouillon cube, cover, bring to a boil, decrease to a simmer, and cook for about 15 minutes. Remove from heat and set aside.

----------- COUSCOUS -----------

Couscous is a bit quicker to make.

※ Mix the bouillon cube in the water as you bring it up to a boil. Remove the boiling water from the heat, add the couscous, stir once and cover. Let this sit for 5 minutes, fluff it with a fork, and set it aside.

----------- EVERYTHING ELSE -----------

※ Cut up the seitan into small pieces, reserve the broth from the package, or from your home-made seitan stash.

※ Heat 1 Tbs oil to medium in a 10-12 inch skillet. Add the seitan, chopped walnuts, and salt. Stir occasionally until the seitan just begins to be browned by the oil.

※ Add the diced red bell pepper and sauté until it is softened, remove this mixture from the heat.

※ In a mixing bowl, combine the cooked quinoa or couscous with the seitan-walnut-pepper mixture.

※ Add the lemon juice, additional oil, black pepper, and chopped basil. Stir everything together, and that's it! So tasty!

Baked Seitan or a Tofurky! with Cranberry Onion Relish

2 Cups of seitan (about 2 packages premade)
vegetable oil, fresh rosemary,
+ fresh ground black pepper, garlic powder, poultry seasoning
[-OR- one thawed Tofurky roast]

2 Tbs canola or olive oil	<-- Relish Part
1 medium onion, diced small	
1 Cup dried cranberries	inspired by a recipe from a(nother) Tofurky fan. In my opinion, the best way to cook a Tofurky, hands down!
2 Tbs brown sugar	
2 tsp dijon mustard	
2 Tbs balsamic vinegar	
4 Tbs apple sauce or apple cider	

SEITAN: Cut the seitan into pieces. In a 10-12 inch skillet, sauté in a bit of oil with a few shakes of the spices, and about 2 tsp of fresh chopped rosemary.

RELISH: In a separate skillet, on medium heat, sauté cranberries & onion in oil until the onion softens some. Add the brown sugar, and stir. Decrease the heat to medium-low and add the mustard, vinegar, and apple. Simmer for a couple of minutes and then remove from heat.

BAKE: grease the bottom of a 9x9 inch pan and place the seitan in the pan with the cranberry mixture on top. Cover the pan with foil and bake for 40 minutes at 350°F. Remove foil and bake 10 minutes more.

FOR A TOFURKY: Make sure it's thawed. Pour the cranberry relish over it, cover the pan with foil, and bake at 350°F for 1 hour & 15 minutes. Uncover and bake another 10 minutes.

Chana Masala

2 Cans chickpeas (garbanzo beans), drained,
with <u>liquid set aside</u>
1 1/2 inch piece of fresh ginger, peeled & grated
1 large onion, finely chopped
3 garlic cloves, minced
1 Tbs lemon juice
2-3 Tbs tomato paste
1/2 to 1 tsp salt (to taste)

PREPARE BATSMATI
or JASMINE
RICE TO GO
WITH THIS DISH
WHILE COOKING.

OTHER SPICES ->

1 tsp garam masala   1 tsp cumin
2 tsp coriander   1/2 tsp turmeric
1/4 tsp cayenne powder   1 tsp amchur*
2 Tbs vegetable oil

DIRECTIONS: Heat oil with spices, ginger, & garlic first.
Then, add onion, tomato paste, lemon juice, and finally about
1 cup of the left-over bean liquid. Allow to SIMMER briefly.
Next, add the chickpeas and stir. Cook covered for about 20
minutes. When ready, the chickpeas will have soaked in the
flavor of the sauce and will be tasty all the way through
🥣 SERVE with RICE. Garnish with fresh tomatoes

...and cilantro if you're feeling fancy.

* You may need to go to an Asian grocery for amchur.

CURRY TOFU & PEAS

MAIN STUFF

1 lb firm tofu
1/2 medium onion, diced
2 to 3 cups frozen green peas
1/4 cup chopped cashews (optional)
some coconut milk, to taste (optional)

> IMPORTANT: the key to this recipe is heating the spices in the oil first. Don't overlook this.

SPICES, ETC:

about 1 Tbs vegetable oil
1 tsp curry powder
1 tsp salt (or to taste)
1 tsp turmeric
4 cloves minced garlic
a few dashes of black pepper

> The spice amounts are approximations. Add more if you like, or less. For a creamier twist, add the coconut milk too.

Serve with RICE -> Cook 1/2 cup dry, prepared according to variety, while making the rest of the dish.

DIRECTIONS:

Heat oil in skillet with the spices FIRST. Once hot & mixed, add tofu, sauté it with the spices, and then add onions. Stir often for about 5 minutes. Then add the peas and sauté another 5 minutes. If you are adding coconut milk, add it to your preference next. Add cashews last, mix in and remove from heat. Mix with rice (or place on top of rice) & serve.

CRUNCHY BROCCOLI SALAD

Main part:
5 Cups chopped raw broccoli florets
1/2 Cup unsalted peanuts
1/4 Cup red onion, diced small
3/4 Cup raisins

Dressing Part:
1/2 Cup vegan mayonnaise
1/4 Cup sugar
2 Tbs red wine vinegar
(or rice vinegar)
1/2 tsp lemon juice

☆ Rinse and then chop the broccoli into bite-size floret pieces. Dice the red onion and rinse the pieces well with cold water in a fine mesh strainer to mellow the raw onion flavor.

☆ In a large mixing bowl, combine the broccoli, peanuts (preferably unsalted, but salted will be ok), rinsed onion, and raisins. Set aside.
☆ In a smaller bowl, mix the dressing ingredients. Whisk everything together until creamy and well blended.
☆ Add the dressing to the broccoli mixture and serve right away. This salad keeps well for about a day in the fridge. On the second leftover day, it will taste fine but smell less great. Make sure to eat it up pretty quickly.

SUSHI ROLLS

2 Cups sushi/pearl rice
2 1/2 Cups water
2 tsp sugar
2 Tbs rice vinegar

1 Package of nori (about 6 sheets)
wasabi paste
tamari + pickled ginger

1 large carrot
1 red bell pepper (optional)

place veggies here

↑
wasabi line
(sushi mat makes tight —
rolling easier)

1 cucumber
1 ripe organic avocado

1/2 lb tofu cut in small/thin strips &
    fried in oil and tamari

👁 Rinse the rice in a fine mesh strainer, then add it to a pot
with the water. Bring this to the start of a boil, reduce heat
to low, cover, & simmer for 15-20 minutes. Remove from heat
and let sit covered. Check that the rice is soft. Cut vegetables
into thin slivers. Steam carrots & pepper over water for 3-5
minutes.
👁 WET HANDS and spread a thin layer of rice onto the nori
sheets. Add a line of veggies, including wasabi (see above). Roll
tightly (with wet hands) and slice each roll into 6 pieces. Serve
with tamari (soy sauce), wasabi paste, and pickled ginger.

Summertime PLUS!
BLACK BEANS & CORN 4-6 SERVINGS

2 (15oz.) cans black beans, strained & rinsed, and simmered
2 ears fresh sweet corn, boiled 10-15 min, & then kernels
  cut off the cobs
1 medium onion, chopped
1 small yellow squash, chopped
1 large carrot, sliced & julienned
1/2 green bell pepper, chopped
1/2 red bell pepper, chopped
2 medium garden tomatoes, diced
2 tsp vegetable oil
+ lettuce & 1/2 organic, ripe avocado

SPICES (use dashes of all, to taste):
  garlic powder, black pepper, chili powder, cumin, ground
  mustard, oregano, pinch of ginger, and Bragg Aminos.

o o o o o o o o o o o o

WHILE boiling corn, sauté all vegetables together in oil with
spices and Bragg Aminos, to desired flavor. Once softened,
remove from heat and mix in cooked black beans.

🥣 SERVE layered on a bed of lettuce & tortilla chips with
the fresh corn (if substituting frozen corn, defrost & cook
completely first). Top with fresh tomatoes and sliced avocado.

Grilled Marinated Portobellos

2 portobello mushroom caps, washed
2 cloves garlic, chopped or minced
about 1 inch fresh ginger, peeled & grated
1 1/2 Tbs vegetarian Worchestershire sauce
4 Tbs tamari
1 tsp lemon juice
1-2 Tbs olive oil
1 tsp fresh rosemary, chopped
2 tsp brown sugar
dash of pepper
+ Onion, peppers, buns or bread, lettuce & tomato.

Wash mushrooms and then smush garlic into the gills on their undersides. Mix all other marinade ingredients and then pour this over mushroom caps in a shallow bowl or pan. Let the mushrooms sit for about 30 minutes, turning and spooning the marinade over them occasionally.

While marinating, prepare grill (or oven, to broil inside). Cut up onions & peppers, and toss them with olive oil, lemon juice, salt & pepper, and rosemary to also grill. Grill mushrooms & veggies for about 5 minutes on each side. Serve as sandwiches with grilled buns/bread, lettuce, tomatoes, and veggies.

Mmmm, mmm, mm!

BEANS&RICE&TVP!

2 15oz cans chili beans
 (seasoned pinto beans in chili sauce)
1/2 Cup rice (dry) - cooked per variety instructions
1/2 green bell pepper, diced
1/2 red bell pepper, diced
1/2 Cup corn (fresh or frozen)
1 medium tomato, diced
1/2 large onion, diced
1/2 Cup TVP (optional)
     rehydrated in 1/2 Cup
     warm/hot water

FIRSTLY: cook the rice and rehydrate the TVP.

SECONDLY: while rice cooks, cut up the vegetables.

1 Tbs vegetable oil
1 tsp chili powder
1/2 tsp black pepper
1/2 tsp dry oregano
1/4 tsp cumin powder
1 tsp Bragg Aminos
1 tsp cornstarch + 1.5 Tbs water
Optional: 1/4 Cup chopped
                cilantro

THIRDLY: In a large skillet, sauté onion & peppers in oil on medium heat, adding spices, for 5-7 minutes. Add corn & TVP and a bit more oil and sauté 5 more minutes.

FOURTHLY: Add chili beans with sauce and tomato. Reduce heat to low.

LASTLY: Mix cornstarch with 1.5 Tbs cold water in a small bowl, & whisk. Add to the skillet & let simmer 2-3 min. Add rice, mix, and serve with cilantro garnish if desired.

☆ MAKES 4 SERVINGS.

Bean Enchiladas✳

SAUCE

* 1 (10 oz.) can mild enchilada sauce
* 1 (6 oz.) can tomato paste
* 1/2 jalapeño pepper, minced
* 2 large cloves garlic, minced
* 1 Tbs dry oregano
  1 tsp coriander
  2 tsp cumin
  2 tsp chili powder

* 3 1/2 Cups water
* 2 tsp vegetable oil
* 1 med. onion, minced

1 Tbs sugar
1/2 tsp black pepper
1 tsp salt
2 tsp Bragg Aminos

-> Make sauce in medium sauce pan – combine all ingredients, cook at a simmer for 25 minutes, uncovered.

FILLING

* 2 (15 oz.) cans pinto beans
* 1 medium onion, diced
* 1 medium green bell pepper, diced

* 2 medium tomatoes, diced
* 1 1/2 Cups corn

-> Sauté vegetables in a bit of oil & chili powder. Remove from heat and mix with beans.

* 10 medium sized corn tortillas

-> Cover the bottom of a 9x13 inch roasting/baking pan with some of the sauce. Heat a 10 inch skillet and fry each tortilla in oil for a few seconds on each side, dip it in the enchilada sauce, fill with "filling," roll up, and place crease-down into the pan. Repeat this for all 10 tortillas. Pour sauce over tortillas, saving some to use after baking.
-> Bake <u>covered</u> with foil for 25 min. at 350°F.
-> Remove from oven and pour the rest of the sauce on top.

PASTA SALAD #1

16 oz rainbow rotini pasta

Veggies:
1/2 green bell pepper, diced
1/2 red or yellow bell pepper, diced
1 medium tomato, diced
1 small cucumber, sliced & chopped
1 small carrot, grated
1 Cup red cabbage, shredded
1 small red or sweet onion, diced
(add other veggies if you like
   such as broccoli...)

Seasonings:
3+ Tbs Nayonaise (or other vegan mayo)
1 Tbs olive oil
2 Tbs balsamic vinegar
   (or more, to taste)
2 Tbs sugar

Approximately 1/2 tsp of the following spices:
   black pepper, garlic powder, coriander,
   celery seed, dry basil, lemon pepper.
   Also add a dash of salt.

2 Tbs sunflower seeds
1/2 Cup sesame sticks

SECRET INGREDIENTS = Coriander + sesame sticks. Yesss!

♡   ♡   ♡

DIRECTIONS:
Cook pasta and rinse
to cool. Set aside.

Cut up the veggies & add
them to a large bowl.

Add the seasonings,
spices, and sunflower
seeds, but not the
sesame sticks. Mix well.

Next, add in the pasta &
mix. Taste and adjust.
Refrigerate.

Wait to add the sesame
sticks until you are
ready to serve if you
want them to stay
crunchy.

Jazzy Ladys Pasta Salad
(QUICKER THAN THE OTHER ONE)

2-3 Cups rainbow (dry) rotini pasta
    * cooked, rinsed, & cooled with cold water
1 medium tomato, diced
1/4-1/2 Cup green bell pepper, diced
1/4-1/2 Cup red/yellow bell pepper, diced
1/4 Cup red onion, finely diced
1/2 small cucumber, peeled & chopped

TO GO!

OTHER POSSIBLE VEGETABLES TO ADD OR SUBSTITUTE:
    -> grated carrot, red cabbage, & broccoli are also good!
3-4 slices veggie "salami" lunch "meat" cut into tiny **O**s
black pepper, to taste
1/3 to 1/2 Cup low-fat prepared dairy-free Italian or
                         vinaigrette salad dressing

While the pasta cooks, chop up the vegetables. Rinse the
chopped onion in a mesh strainer with cold water to cut down
on its raw pungency.
Toss veggies + veggie "salami" together in a medium mixing bowl
and coat with salad dressing. Add pasta & pepper.
Mix together and refrigerate.

Makes 2-3 servings amd takes 20 min. or less to prepare!

Fresh Falafel

1 15 oz can garbanzo beans (chickpeas), drained
1 Cup onion, finely minced
1 Tbs minced garlic
1/4 Cup flour
1/2 tsp baking powder
2 Tbs dried parsley
1 tsp cumin
1 tsp coriander
1/2 tsp paprika
1/4 tsp black pepper
1/2 tsp salt
olive or canola oil

----

2 Tbs tahini
1 tsp lemon juice
4 tsp water

----

diced tomato
sliced cucumber
lettuce +

----

rice vinegar
hummus
pita bread

DIRECTIONS:

1. Drain and rinse the beans well. Mash them with a fork or potato masher, or chop them coarsely in a food processor. Mix in onion, garlic, flour, baking powder, and spices. Let this mixture sit for a few minutes, then form it into balls or patties and either deep-fry in heated oil, or fry in a small amount of oil, turning to cook both sides (better for small patties and my preferred method).

2. Mix tahini with water and lemon to form a creamy sauce that pours.

----

3. Toss lettuce in rice vinegar.
4. Serve the falafel in pita bread with tomato, lettuce, cucumber, tahini, and hummus. Ooh yum!
And not from a box!

Balsamic Veggies & Potatoes FOR ONE

① Boil or bake 1 medium potato until soft
   (Boiling will have a moister result)

② Sauté vegetables in a large pan with olive oil:
   - 1/2 small red onion, diced
   - 1/2 red bell or sweet Italian pepper, cut up
   - 1/2 green bell pepper, cut up
   - 1/2 zucchini or yellow squash, cut in rounds
   - Other veggies? steamed green beans, carrot...

③ Add spices & seasoning:
   → a few dashes of black pepper, basil, salt, garlic.

④ Once the vegetables have softened and browned, remove the
   pan from heat and add about 1 Tbs balsamic vinegar. Mix in.

⑤ Either cut up the potato and sauté it with the vegetables
   before serving, <or> cut the potato in its skin and serve
   the veggies on top of it.

Serve with vegetarian Worchestershire sauce or a
vinaigrette salad dressing.

Hearty and wholesome

CORNBREAD

1 1/2 Cups finely ground cornmeal

1/2 Cup whole wheat flour   PREHEAT OVEN TO 425°F

1 tsp baking powder

1 tsp baking soda   2 Tbs maple syrup or 4 tsp molasses

3/4 tsp salt   2 Tbs canola oil

- - - - - -

1 Tbs ground flax seed blended with 3 Tbs warm water
(or other single egg substitution, such as Ener-G or Bob's)

1 1/2 Cups plain soymilk or other grain/nut milk

3 Tbs unsweetened applesauce

- - - - - -

for pan: 2-3 tsp vegan margarine

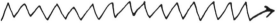

** Mix dry ingredients and wet ingredients separately and then add them to the dry part, stirring gently.

** Add 2-3 tsp vegan margarine to 10 inch cast iron skillet or 9x9 inch baking pan and pre-heat the pan in the oven for several minutes until hot.

** Remove the hot pan or skillet to the stovetop, pour in the batter, and then put it back in the oven to bake for 20-25 minutes @ 425°F until the top is browned and your test knife comes out clean.

shepherd's pie with lentils

Fancy!

PRE-COOKING THE LENTILS PART:
2 Cups dry brown lentils, rinsed
>   5 cups of water
>   1/2 no-salt vegetable bouillon cube
>   1 bay leaf
>   1/4 tsp garlic powder, or so
>   1 medium white or yellow onion, chopped

MASHED POTATOES PART:
3 large russet or red potatoes, or several smaller potatoes
>   Several cups of water to boil the potatoes
>   3/4 Cup warmed plain soymilk
>   2 tsp vegan margarine
>   garlic powder, salt, and pepper, to taste

FINISHING UP THE LENTILS PART:
1 tsp salt
1/2 tsp oregano
1/2 tsp sage powder
3 cloves garlic, minced
dash of: cayenne pepper, black pepper, & celery seed
<u>one drop</u> of liquid smoke flavoring, or a dash of veg. smoke
flavor powder

Coming up:

TWO
LAYER
GOODNESS

Directions for making your impressive Shepherd's Pie

PRE-COOKING THE LENTILS

--> In a medium-large saucepan, heat 5 cups of water with the lentils, bay leaf, bouillon cube, and garlic, bringing the heat up to a low boil and then down to a simmer for 20 minutes. Then, add the chopped onion, and simmer 5-10 more minutes. Set aside.

MAKING THE MASHED POTATOES

--> In a separate pan, boil potatoes (cut up) until soft, 15-20 minutes. Remove from heat and drain off water. Mash the potatoes with the soymilk, margarine, garlic, salt, and pepper. Set aside.

* Preheat oven to 400°F *

FINISHING UP THE LENTILS A LITTLE BIT MORE

--> Wash off your potato masher and now use it to mash up the lentils. Add the spices and seasonings and mix well (If you used a salted bouillon cube, use less or no salt in this part).

PUTTING IT ALL TOGETHER!

--> Place the lentil mash mixture into the bottom of a 9x13 inch baking pan, flattening it out into an even layer.

--> Place the mashed potatoes on top of the lentils next, spreading them out gently into a second, top layer.

--> Bake for 20 minutes at 400°F

--> Switch the oven to broil, and broil for no more than 5 minutes to brown the top. It might take less than 5 minutes, so keep your attention on the progress. Cool a bit, and then eat!

WINTERTIME "STUFFING"

8 Cups of wheat bread cubes (baguette or other dense bread)
→ dried out in a pan in a 250°F Oven for 40-50 minutes
<<OR>>
1 recipe of cornbread cooled & crumbled into large bowl

- - - - - -

1 1/2 Cups vegetable broth (1 veg. bouillon cube dissolved into
1 1/4 Cup chopped celery   1 1/2 Cups hot water)
1 medium onion, minced
4 cloves fresh garlic, minced
spices: 1/4 tsp sage powder   1/2 tsp thyme
                  3/4 tsp black pepper   1/2 tsp salt
1 Tbs vegetable oil
1/4 Cup plain soymilk

DIRECTIONS: Sauté the onion and garlic in oil on medium heat
for 5 minutes. Add celery and sauté for a couple more minutes.

IN A CASSEROLE dish or roasting pan, mix the bread with the
vegetable broth & spices. Mix in vegetables & soymilk. Let sit
in fridge overnight for best results. Add a little more water
before baking if you have let the dish rest in this way.
BAKE, covered with foil for 1 hour at 300°F. Remove foil for
the last 10 minutes to brown the top, if desired.

Absolutely Fabulous WILD RICE

米 RICE

*FOR TWO
SERVINGS

1 Cup wild rice blend
1/2 or 1 vegetable bouillon cube
2 1/4 Cups water
1 tsp vegetable oil
2-3 dashes of tamari (or soy sauce)
1-2 tsp Bragg Aminos, if you have some
ADD DASHES of the following spices:
  black pepper, paprika, celery seed, + dry basil.
ALSO ADD
3 cloves fresh garlic, minced
2 slices of sweet onion, diced
2 celery sticks, chopped

DIRECTIONS: Start the rice in water with the bouillon cube on high heat, briefly, and turn down to a simmer when it starts to boil. As soon as you put the rice in, quickly cut up the garlic and veggies and add them. Add some spices and let simmer mostly-covered, but not completely covered, for about 40 minutes total.
When the rice is done, there should be some liquid left and the rice should be tender/soft.

BLACK BEANS and YAMS

to serve over rice, or yellow/blue corn tortilla chips

1 (15oz) can black beans
  (= 1 1/2 Cup cooked beans + 1/2 Cup water)
1 large garnet yam, cubed
1-2 tsp vegetable oil
1/2 medium white or yellow onion, chopped
1 clove garlic, minced
1 small or medium tomato, diced
chili powder & garlic powder
3+ Tbs mild or medium salsa

* If you're serving this with rice, start cooking 1/2 cup (dry) of brown or long-grain white rice as specified for that variety.
* In a saucepan, simmer the can of beans with the liquid (saltier) or strain and rinse the beans first and add 1/2 cup water (less salt) on medium-low heat. Add a few dashes of garlic & chili powder to the beans to season them.
* Wash, peel, and cut up the yam and then steam it in a pot with a steam basket or insert for about 10 minutes maximum.
* Meanwhile, in a skillet, sauté the onion & garlic in oil until the onion softens. Add the tomato briefly and remove from heat.
* When all three parts are done, layer them together to serve over rice or tortilla chips, adding the fresh salsa on top, last.

Broccolini
to die for

6 stalks of broccolini, rinsed
1/2 Cup vegetable broth
2 tsp olive oil
2-3 medium garlic cloves, minced
fresh ground black pepper, to taste
salt, to taste

for 1 big portion
or 2 small portions

EASY and FLAVORFUL!

❧ Trim the ends of the cut broccolini and remove the leaves.

❧ Add vegetable broth, garlic, and oil to a 10 inch stainless steel pan. Bring this mixture to a simmer and then add the broccolini stalks, distributing them evenly in the pan.

❧ Cover the pan to simmer the broccolini for about 2 1/2 minutes - turn the broccolini onto their other side and simmer about another 2 1/2 minutes.

❧ Remove from heat once the broccolini has softened and turned a bright, deeper green. Be careful not to over cook the pieces. serve al dente with the broth.

SMOKY TEMPEH & KALE

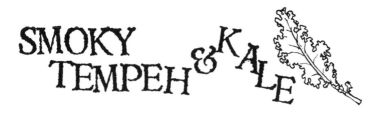

1 8oz tempeh cake
6 big leafy stalks of green or purple kale, chopped

Marinade

4 Tbs low-salt tamari
1 tsp liquid smoke
2 Tbs maple syrup or molasses
2 Tbs rice vinegar
2 Tbs safflower oil (or sesame, canola or refined olive oil)
1 Tbs no-salt or low-salt vegetable broth (optional)
1/4 tsp paprika
1/2 tsp sage powder
2 tsp nutritional yeast flakes
Pinch of cayenne powder
1/8 tsp ground black pepper
2 large cloves garlic, minced
1 Tbs minced onion

This marinated tempeh is so good it gets to have two pages. Oh yeah.

PRE-BOIL and MARINATE

◎ Start by boiling the tempeh for 15 minutes in about 5 cups of water. Add one no-salt veg. bouillon cube for more flavor.

◎ In a large bowl, combine the marinade ingredients and whisk them together.

◎ After simmering, remove the tempeh & set the water (or broth) aside.

◎ Slice the tempeh into 1/4-1/2 inch strips.

   * If using for sandwiches, leave in thin strips.

   * Otherwise, cut the tempeh further into shorter, bite-sized pieces.

◎ Place the tempeh in the marinade, turn it and coat it well, and let it marinate for at least 20 minutes.

THEN, BAKE

◎ Pre-heat the oven to 375°F with a 9x13 in. baking pan inside. Once at temp., place the tempeh in the pan & return to the oven.

◎ Bake for 10 minutes, switch to broil just until the top is darkened, turn the tempeh over & broil the other side 3-5 min.

OR GRILL!

Grill 1/2 inch or larger pieces on skewers or in a grill basket until browned or slightly blackened. Time will depend on temperature of your grill or flame level.

OR STIR-FRY

◎ Heat skillet to medium. Add tempeh chunks & stir frequently until carmelized.

◎ Add the kale and stir fry it with the tempeh with about 2 Tbs of marinade for only about 2 minutes. Stir constantly.

- - - - -

Serve the tempeh & kale alone, or with rice, or just make the tempeh to use in a sandwich->

Ridiculously ^easy vegan BLT

There was a suggestion on the label of a jar of (soy-based) Bacos artificial bacon bits at one time... I tried it and loved it! Maybe not as good for salt-sensitive folks, but it's very easy for a quick lunch. If you've got more time, try the smoky tempeh instead!

2 SLICES OF TOASTED BREAD

Half of a smallish, ripe tomato, sliced

About 2 Tbs of Nayonaise, Vegenaise, or other vegan mayo-style dressing

Approximately 1/4 Cup Bacos chips, bits, or other similar artificial soy/wheat "bacon" bits product

A nice piece of lettuce

DIRECTIONS: Toast the bread, spread the vegan mayo, and then distribute the bacon bits evenly around your bottom piece of toast. Add lettuce and tomato to finish up the sandwich! Instead of Bacos, also try: My smoky tempeh recipe of course! Also, Lightlife's smoky tempeh Fakin' Bacon strips and Smart Bacon strips are super yummy!

because I so like "Jeff's Cheesy Bowties" from the Corvallis First Alternative Co-op, and this is kinda like that...

2 Cups small pasta (shells, bowties, macaroni) ☆
2 Tbs extra virgin olive oil ☆
2-3 Tbs nutritional yeast flakes ☆
1 Tbs balsamic vinegar ☆
1/4 tsp garlic powder ☆
1/8 tsp salt ☆
1/8 tsp fresh ground black pepper ☆
☆ 1/3 Cup red onion, minced
☆ 1 to 1 1/2 Cups chopped fresh spinach
☆ 1 Cup ripe tomatoes, diced

Boil the two cups of pasta, strain, and rinse.
☞ Transfer the pasta to a mixing bowl, and while still warm, add the olive oil, nutritional yeast, and balsamic vinegar. Stir well until the pasta is well coated. Add the garlic, salt, and pepper and mix.
☞ Chop the onion finely and then rinse it well using a fine mesh strainer. Chop the spinach into small pieces - use a sharp knife to avoid bruising. Rinse the seeds from the tomatoes and dice them.
☞ Finally, combine the veggies with the pasta and stir until they are well incorporated.

CRISPY ★ ROASTED ★ POTATOES

8 Cups red potatoes - washed and cut into 3/4 to 1 inch cubes
3-4 Tbs canola or safflower oil
fresh ground black pepper
fresh rosemary
salt
Preheat oven to 425°F

☕ Prepare stock pot with steamer insert or tray and steam the potatoes for 5 minutes. Remove, and allow the potatoes to cool uncovered for a few minutes, while prepping pans.

☞ Put about 2 Tbs of oil in each of two 9x13 inch roasting pans; Place both pans in the pre-heated oven to heat up for about 5 minutes.

Once the pans and oil are nice and hot, bring them to the stove top, quickly put half of the potatoes in each pan and stir around a bit (the potatoes should sizzle).

⟶ Sprinkle pepper, salt, and fresh rosemary over the potatoes and put them back in the oven.

Bake for <u>35 minutes</u>, stir and turn the potatoes, then return to the oven and bake <u>10-25 minutes longer.</u> Longer cooking time will result in very crispy and browned potatoes, but I like them best that way! Check yours often after 45 minutes of cooking so they end up just how you want them!

BAKED POTATO FRIES

* 1 giant, or 2 med. potatoes
* vegetable oil
* salt
* pepper
* paprika
* Ketchup or BBQ sauce

① Cut potatoes into fry-shaped pieces.

② Preheat oven to 425°F

③ Soak potatoes in cold water for 15 minutes and then drain & dry off with a towel.

④ Place fries in a bowl and pour a couple of teaspoons of oil over them. Add spices and salt & mix with hands. Spread the fries onto a baking sheet in a single layer.

⑤ Bake for about 15 minutes, flip over with spatula, and then bake for another 15 minutes. ⟶
(Baking time will depend on how thick or thin you made your fries. Keep an eye on them and remove early if necessary.)

These are not nearly as unhealthy as deep fried french fries. They take a while to make, but are a nice treat.
Also try this recipe using sweet potatoes or yams. If you use yams, rinse them, but you don't need to soak them.

179

Nutritional Yeast Cheese

1/2 Cup nutritional yeast flakes
1/2 Cup unbleached flour
1 tsp salt
1/2-3/4 tsp garlic powder
2 Cups water
1/4 Cup vegan margarine
1/2 tsp wet mustard
FOR SPICY DIP, ALSO ADD:
     1/2 to 1 tsp chili powder or paprika
     1/2 tsp black pepper

EASY ALTERNATIVE FOR GRILLED "CHEESE" SANDWICHES OR "NACHO CHEESE" DIP!

DIRECTIONS:
☙ combine dry ingredients in a sauce pan. Whisk together, add water, and mix well while heating stove to medium.
Stir often until this begins to thicken. Add margarine and mustard, stirring as the margarine melts. Continue to stir a few more minutes until sufficiently thickened.
☙ For spicy dip, add additional spices and serve hot.
☙ For sandwiches, refrigerate until stiff. "Butter" the out-sides of your bread slices, spread the "cheese" on the inside, add a little bit of fresh ground pepper, and fry in a skillet on medium heat until both sides are browned.
☙ Not exactly like cheese, but yummy in its own way!

Vegans subsisting only
on sugar do not set a
very good example, so
don't admit it if this
describes you.

On the other hand, if you
bake your own sweets at
least they'll be healthier
than some of those
"technically vegan"
grocery options.

"Oops, I ate the whole pan"
cancels out "healthier,"
so please note that both
halving and sharing these
recipes is easy!

Sweets

BANANA
BREAD

USE ORGANIC
THEY ARE NICER

Wet ingredients
4 small or 2-3 large, very ripe bananas
1 1/2 tsp vanilla extract
1/3 Cup melted vegan margarine
1 egg replacement - Ener-G or ground flax, see ingredient tips
1/2 Cup sugar   section
1/2 Cup brown sugar
dry ingredients
1 3/4 Cups all-purpose flour   1/2 tsp allspice
1 tsp baking soda   1 tsp cinnamon
1 tsp baking powder
last ingredients
* extra brown sugar to sprinkle on top *
1/2 Cup chopped walnuts (optional)

PREHEAT OVEN TO 325°F

Mash the bananas with thoroughness. A potato masher works
splendidly for this task.
Next: add the other wet ingredients and sugars, and mix well.
Sift together flour, baking powder & baking soda, and then
add all of the dry ingredients to the bowl. Stir gently until the
batter is all mixed. Ta Da! Add nuts now, if you want them.
Pour the batter into a lightly greased & floured bread pan, and
sprinkle brown sugar on top. (Very important last step!)
BAKE FOR about 50 MINUTES at 325°F (Check w/knife to be
sure when it's done).   Mmmm...

ZUCCHINI BREAD

Zucchini bread is similar to banana bread and other spiced quick breads

1/3 Cup vegetable oil
1 1/2 egg replacements
  (Ener-G egg replacer works well)
1/2 Cup sugar
1/2 Cup brown sugar
1 tsp vanilla
- - - - - - - - - - -

1 1/2 Cups + 2 Tbs unbleached or whole wheat pastry flour
1/2 tsp salt
1/2 tsp cinnamon
1/2 tsp nutmeg
1/2 tsp baking powder
1 1/2 tsp baking soda
- - - - - - - - - - -

1 Cup peeled and grated zucchini

PREHEAT OVEN TO 350°F

Mix the wet ingredients (except for zucchini) and sugars in one bowl, and the dry ingredients together, separately, in another. Whisk the dry ingredients to mix well. Combine the two mixtures and stir gently to form a batter. Mix in the grated zucchini last. POUR the batter into a greased & floured bread pan and BAKE at 350°F for about 45-50 minutes.
  (test w/knife after 45 minutes to see if it's done)

≡MOM'S OATMEAL SPICE CAKE

1 Cup quick oats (uncooked)
1 1/4 Cups boiling water
1/2 Cup vegan margarine
2 egg replacements
3/4 Cup sugar
1 Cup brown sugar

1 1/2 Cups flour
  (whole wheat pastry or white)
1/2 tsp baking soda
1 tsp baking powder
1 tsp cinnamon
1/2 tsp ground cloves
1/2 tsp salt

"Cream Cheese" Glaze
*4 oz Better Than Cream
  Cheese Tofutti
*Powdered sugar–add a
  few teaspoons at a time
*Water, about 1 tsp, if
  needed.
Mix until glaze has the
desired sweetness and
pour over your cake.
  Yum!

--> In a large mixing bowl, combine oatmeal, hot water, and margarine. Let this sit for 10 minutes, or until the margarine is melted.

. . . .

NEXT: Stir in egg replacer (see ingredient tips), sugars, and then the dry ingredients – flour, baking powder, spices, salt.

. . . .

* Pour batter into a greased & floured 9x13 inch pan or equivalent. Bake for 45 minutes @ 350°F.
Sprinkle baked cake with powdered sugar –or– make "cream cheese" glaze described in box above top –or– use store-bought artificial "cream cheese" frosting (Pillsbury makes one).

Carrot Cake

3 Ener-G egg replacements
1/2 Cup white sugar
1 Cup brown sugar
1/3 Cup vegetable oil
2/3 Cup plain soymilk
2 1/2 Cups unbleached flour

1 tsp baking soda
1 tsp baking powder
1 1/2 tsp cinnamon
1 1/2 tsp allspice
1 1/2 Cups grated carrots

Optional: 1/2 Cup chopped walnuts; 1/4 tsp ground cloves

PREHEAT YOUR OVEN TO 350°F

Whisk the egg replacer & water in a small bowl (see box & ingredient tips). Then, in a medium mixing bowl, mix that with oil, soymilk, and sugars.

Gently fold in flour, baking soda, baking powder, & spices until blended.

Lastly, fold in the grated carrots – and walnuts, if desired. Pour into a greased 9x13 inch cake pan or two 9" round cake pans, if you want to make a layer cake.

BAKE at 350° F for 35 minutes.

Ice the cake once it cools with "cream cheese" icing. Use either Tofutti "cream cheese" to make a glaze (see Oatmeal Spice Cake recipe), or use store-bought totally artificially flavored frosting.

(Pillsbury makes a delicious, not very healthful, but technically vegan, "cream cheese" frosting, if you're okay with that).

SPECIAL CHOCOLATE CAKE

aka wacky cake!

1 1/2 Cups unbleached flour
1 Cup sugar
3 Tbs dutch cocoa powder
1 tsp baking soda
1 tsp vanilla extract
5 Tbs vegetable oil
1 Cup cold water
1 Tbs white vinegar
1/2 Cup vegan chocolate chips

This Cake is nice & moist, and good with Chocolate frosting AND with fresh strawberries.

PREHEAT OVEN TO 350° F

🍲 Mix together flour, sugar, cocoa, and baking soda. Next, add the oil, vanilla, and water, mix well, add the vinegar last.
🍲 Blend until creamy. Pour the batter into a greased 8x8 or 9x9 inch pan, and sprinkle chocolate chips around on top of the batter.

BAKE at 350°F for 30-35 minutes or until center is done (check with a knife). Allow to cool and then add chocolate frosting.

Also great for cupcakes! They'll require a shorter baking time, so for cupcakes bake for about 20 minutes.

Home-Made Chocolate Frosting

3 Tbs dutch cocoa powder (or 3 oz unsweetened chocolate)
2 tsp vegan margarine
1/4 Cup hot water or heated ricemilk
1 tsp vanilla extract
2+ cups powdered sugar

Over low heat, melt the margarine & cocoa together. Add water
& vanilla. Remove from heat and stir in the sugar until the
frosting gets thick and creamy. A simple frosting option.

ALTERNATE FUDGE FROSTING ☆ ☆

INGREDIENTS:

3 Cups sugar
1 1/2 Cups soymilk or ricemilk
1/4 Cup dutch cocoa powder
1/2 tsp salt
2 tsp vanilla
2 tsp vegan margarine

(Makes more than the above
recipe)

-Stir & cook sugar, soymilk,
cocoa, & salt over medium heat
until a boil starts.
-Boil while stirring constantly
for 2 minutes until the mix is
thick and drips slowly from
spoon.
-Remove from heat and add the
vanilla & margarine,
 mixing for several minutes.
                Spread!
(best for cake)

Chocolate Buttercream ☆ Frosting

For a full recipe of cupcakes

1/2 Cup cold vegan (baking) margarine
1/4 Cup chilled plain soymilk,
    or, coconut milk, almond milk, or ricemilk

1 1/2 tsp vanilla extract
3 Cups powdered sugar
1/2 Cup (dutch) cocoa powder

electric hand mixer

--> Slice the cold margarine and combine it
in a mixing bowl with the "milk" of choice.
(these have to be cold)
--> carefully beat these together with an electric hand mixer
until they looked creamy and well combined.
--> Once that's done, add the vanilla, about half of the
powdered sugar, and cocoa powder. Beat everything together
with the mixer until incorporated.
--> Add the rest of the sugar and beat until combined. The
frosting should be stiff, not soft.
--> this frosting is for piping! Using a spatula, transfer into a
(large) pastry bag with a cool tip to decorate your cupcakes!

XMAS SUGAR
<FROM MOM>
COOKIES

1/2 Cup vegan margarine
3/4 Cup sugar
1 Ener-G egg replacement

MIX above items & then STIR IN:
1 Tbs plain soymilk
1 Tbs vanilla extract

THEN ADD:
1 1/4 Cups sifted unbleached flour
1/4 tsp baking powder
1/4 tsp salt

PREHEAT OVEN TO 350° F
Mix ingredients in order thoroughly.
Chill dough in the fridge or freezer until firm.
Then, roll out a portion of the dough on a well-floured surface, to about 1/4 inch thickness.
Cut out shapes with cookie cutters. Place cookies onto a lightly greased cookie sheet, and re-chill the remaining dough between batches.

BAKE for 8 Minutes, but keep an eye on the oven since baking time will vary depending on cookie thickness. Adjust baking time based on first batch. Cookies should be light golden brown.

ICING Easy icing can be made by whisking together about 3 Tbs of powdered sugar with 1 tsp water & 1 drop of food coloring.

APPLE CRISP

5 Cups thinly sliced, tart apples
(about 5 small, or 3 large apples)

☆ PART I

1 Tbs unbleached flour
1/2 tsp cinnamon
1/2 Cup sugar
1/2 Cup water

☆ PART II

1 Cup quick oats or rolled oats
3/4 Cup unbleached flour
3/4 Cup brown sugar
1/4 tsp baking powder
1/4 tsp baking soda
1/2 Cup melted vegan margarine

* Serve hot with
vanilla soy ice cream
or pour 1 Tbs or so
of chilled soymilk
over your serving for
added creaminess.

※ Preheat oven. Place apple slices into a greased 9x13" inch pan,
or in two smaller pans.
※ In a small bowl, mix flour, cinnamon, & sugar from Part I.
Sprinkle this over the apples and then pour the water evenly
over the apples also.
※ Combine the Part II ingredients in a separate bowl, mixing
everything together nicely. Sprinkle this over apples in pan.

※ BAKE at 350°F for 45 minutes.   so good!!

Easy Rice Pudding

1 1/2 Cups precooked rice

1/2 tsp cinnamon

2 tsp vanilla extract

1/2 Cup raisins

2 1/2 Tbs sugar

1 Tbs honey (optional, or use additional sugar)

1 tsp vegan margarine

2 Cups plain or vanilla soymilk or rice milk

(Optional variation- add 1 Tbs unsweetened shredded coconut)

Add all the ingredients together in a medium pot, bringing it up to a simmer (low-medium heat). Cook for 20-30 minutes, uncovered, stirring often.

The soymilk/ricemilk will thicken/reduce to a pudding-like consistency when done.

Make a double recipe for a good supply of left-overs for a few days. In the winter holiday season, serve hot with a splash of soy eggnog beverage on top for an added treat. Mmmmm!

BREAD ★ ★
PUDDING ★

2 1/2 Cups old (plain) bread, in cubes
    (artisan bread/baguette is best)
1/2 Cup sugar
1/4 tsp salt
1/2 tsp nutmeg
1/2 tsp cinnamon
a dash of allspice & cloves
1/4 - 1/2 Cup raisins
1/4 Cup melted vegan margarine
2 Cups scalded plain soymilk
2 Ener-G or soy flour egg replacements

Mix this while pudding bakes →

SAUCE:
1/2 Tbs cornstarch
1/2 tsp cold water
1/4 Cup sugar
1/2 Cup hot water
1 Tbs margarine
2 Tbs lemon juice
1/2 tsp lemon zest

PREHEAT OVEN TO 350°F →

* Cut up the bread and set it aside. Combine the other dry ingredients & wet ingredients separately and then mix them together. Add the bread and coat it completely.
* Pour this into an 8x8 inch pan, and place the pan into a larger pan with water in it, reaching up 1/3 of the side of the pan.
* bake this part for 45 minutes at 350°F.
* While that bakes, make the lemon sauce in a saucepan. Mix cornstarch with a small amount of cold water in a separate small bowl, then mix it in with everything else. Stir on medium-low heat, until it thickens.

    --Pour sauce over the baked pudding to complete.--

PEANUT BUTTER COOKIES

1/2 Cup sugar

1/2 Cup brown sugar

1/2 Cup peanut butter

1/2 Cup vegan margarine

3 Tbs water

☆ ☆

1 1/4 Cups unbleached flour (+ more if needed, if too sticky)

1/2 tsp baking soda

3/4 tsp baking powder

1/2 tsp salt

PREHEAT OVEN TO 375°F

First, mix together sugars, margarine, peanut butter, and water.
Separately, mix flour, baking soda & baking powder, and salt.
Mix the 2 groups together.
* Make 1 1/4 inch balls of dough, spacing them out generously on
a cookie sheet.
* Flatten them with a fork that has been re-dipped in flour
each time, making that all-important peanut butter cookie mark.
BAKE at 375°F for 9-10 MINUTES, or until golden brown. For
softer cookies, bake at 350°F for 11 minutes.
Try also with chocolate frosting, or include chocolate chips!

Almond White Cake!

1 Cup warmed-up plain almond milk or rice milk
1/4 Cup melted vegan margarine
2 Tbs canola oil
2 Ener-G egg replacements (mixed)
2 tsp lemon juice
1 tsp pure almond extract   2 Cups unbleached flour
1 Cup sugar   1/2 tsp baking soda
--->   1 tsp baking powder
powdered sugar,   1/2 tsp salt
1/3 Cup slivered almonds (optional)

- - - - - > Be sure to preheat the oven to 350°F! < - - - - -
☞ Mix the wet ingredients and sugar in a large bowl. Beat on medium-low with an electric hand mixer until smooth.
☞ Grease and flour a 9x9 inch baking pan or round springform pan so it's ready to go.
☞ In a separate bowl, sift in the flour, then whisk in the baking soda, baking powder, and salt.
☞ Add the flour mixture to the wet mixture and quickly beat together on medium-low speed until fully mixed and slightly fluffed. Only spend about 30 seconds for this.
☞ Transfer to the baking pan and sprinkle almonds on the top (optional), then BAKE AT 350°F FOR 30-35 MINUTES
* Once done, dust the cake with plenty of powdered sugar, or top with strawberries. Maybe even go all-out and use this cake to make a strawberry shortcake!

Oatmeal-Chocolate Chip Cookies

1/2 Cup oil (or a bit less)
1/2 Cup maple syrup
2 Tbs water
1 Tbs vanilla extract
1 Cup whole wheat flour
dash of salt
1/4 tsp baking soda
3/4 Cup quick oats (or rolled oats)
3/4 Cup unsweetened shredded coconut
1 Cup chocolate chips

PREHEAT
OVEN TO
325°F

☆ ☆ MIX INGREDIENTS TOGETHER... well, except for the coconut and chocolate chips – add them last.

Let the batter sit for a few minutes. The dough will be very sticky. That's OK! Place cookie blobs on a cookie sheet and Bake them for 8-10 minutes at 325°F.

Then, Eat!

Very Tasty!

Whole wheat flour, oats, maple syrup? Healthy cookies! right?

SNICKERDOODLES

1 1/2 Cups sugar
1/2 Cup <u>softened</u> vegan margarine
+ 1/4 Cup vegetable shortening
    (or just use 3/4 Cup margarine)
1 tsp vanilla extract
2 egg replacements
    (Ener-G works well here)

2 3/4 Cups flour
1 tsp cream of tartar
1 tsp baking soda
1/4 tsp salt

– – – – –

2 Tbs sugar
2 tsp cinnamon

* Combine the sugar & wet ingredients first.

* Mix flour and other dry ingredients in gradually. Dough will be very dry and it'll barely hold together.

Mix cinnamon & sugar in a small bowl; roll the dough into small balls to then roll in the sugar mixture.

PREHEAT OVEN TO 400° F
Place cookies about 2 inches apart on a cookie sheet and smush them down a bit to flatten them.
BAKE for 8-10 minutes.

For best results, leave the cookies uncovered overnight – don't put them in a sealed bag or container too quickly or they'll be super crisp!

CHOCOLATE MOUSSE PIE

1 package soft silken tofu
10 oz dairy-free chocolate chips
3 Tbs maple syrup
1 graham cracker crust
  (ready-mades contain honey)

1. Blend the tofu in a blender.
2. Melt the chocolate in a double boiler
(or in a pot sitting in a larger pot of
boiling water).
3. Add maple syrup & chocolate to the
tofu and blend.
4. Pour into the graham cracker crust and chill
for 30 minutes to an hour to set.
For a non-honey alternative, use a pre-cooked vegan
pie crust (see pot pie recipe), or just pour the filling into
custard cups.

CAUTION!
THIS IS EXTREMELY RICH. DON'T EAT TOO MUCH
AT ONCE! DANGEROUS!
ALMOST AS DANGEROUS AS A REAL MOOSE! (ok, not really.)

COCOA NO-BAKE ☆ ☆ ☆ ☆ ☆DROPS ☆

1/2 Cup vegan margarine
1/2 Cup plain or vanilla soymilk or ricemilk
2 Cups (finely granulated) sugar
1/4 Cup dutch cocoa powder
1 tsp vanilla extract
5 Tbs peanut butter (preferably crunchy)
1/4 tsp salt
3 Cups rolled oats (not quick oats)
1/4 Cup dairy-free chocolate chips

makes 24-30 cookies

For best results, if your sugar is coarse, grind it in a food processor to reduce it to a finer texture. Also, prepare to work quickly: measure peanut butter, cocoa, oats, and chocolate chips in advance, and set them aside without mixing them.

1. MELT the margarine in a large saucepan on low heat. Add sugar and soymilk, stir, and increase heat to medium.

2. Bring to a boil for 1-2 minutes to fully dissolve the sugar. Whisk vigorously! Set a timer and <u>only boil for 2 min. max.</u>

3. Remove from heat and quickly add the peanut butter and cocoa. Whisk vigorously until mixture is uniform & fudgy.

4. Quickly! Add the oats & chocolate chips and stir until They're well covered.

5. Quickly! While the mixture is still hot, drop & shape blobs from a spoon onto a cookie sheet lined with parchment paper. Let cookies cool in the fridge until firmed up.

fancy brownies

1/2 Cup vegan margarine, softened
1 1/2 Tbs vegetable oil
1 1/4 Cups sugar
1 package silken tofu (about 1 1/2 Cups)
1 1/2 tsp vanilla
1 1/3 Cups unbleached flour
1/2 Cup unsweetened cocoa   (or) 1/2 Cup dutch cocoa
1/2 tsp baking soda   (or) 1/2 tsp baking powder
3/4 to 1 Cup dairy-free chocolate chips
1/2 Cup walnuts

PREHEAT OVEN TO 350°

DIRECTIONS:
--> Combine margarine, oil, and sugar in a bowl. Add the tofu and vanilla, stir a bit, but then transfer everything to a blender or food processor. BLEND on low until the mixture is well-blended and fluffed up.
--> Whisk together flour, cocoa, and leavening in a bowl (there are two common kinds of cocoa that have different properties, so use either baking soda or baking powder, accordingly).
--> Add in the blended wet mixture, mixing everything together. Last, add chocolate chips & walnuts, and then pour into 9x13 inch lightly oiled pan. BAKE for 20-25 min.

Chocolate Chip Cookies of course!

1 Cup brown sugar
1/2 Cup white sugar
3/4 Cup vegan margarine, melted
2 tsp vanilla extract
2 Ener-G egg replacements*
2 Cups unbleached flour
3 Tbs soy protein powder
  (or substitute with additional flour)
1 Tbs powdered soymilk*
1/2 tsp baking powder
1 1/4 Cups dairy-free chocolate chips

PREHEAT OVEN
TO 350° F

DIRECTIONS : Blend margarine, egg replacements, sugar, and vanilla first. Then add flour with soy powder, baking powder, & soymilk powder. The dough should be smooth but neither super-sticky nor cakey. Add a bit more flour if the dough is a little too sticky. Last, add the chocolate chips. Chill the dough briefly in the fridge or freezer and between batches. Make 2-3 inch diameter cookies on baking pan and bake at 350°F for about 9-10 minutes. Take out of the oven when edges are browned, but the tops aren't. Cool them on a cooling rack. These taste even better several hours to a day after baking.

* Refer to the ingredient tips section.

Banana-Oat Cookies

USE ORGANIC BANANAS — THEY ARE NICER.

I Cup pureed banana (about 2 small, very ripe bananas)
1/2 Cup + 2 Tbs vegan margarine, melted
1 Tbs vanilla extract

_____

3 Cups old fashioned rolled oats -or- quick oats
1 Cup unbleached flour or whole wheat pastry flour
1 1/4 Cups sugar
1/2 tsp salt
2 tsp baking powder

_____

PREHEAT OVEN TO 350° F ☆

Combine the wet and dry ingredients separately.
Then, mix these two groups together. Refrigerate the dough for
a few minutes while the oven heats up.

Make cookie-sized blobs on a cookie sheet and bake for 12
minuntes, until cookies are slightly golden brown. Allow the
cookies to cool on wax paper or parchment paper. They will be
flimsy and won't do well on a rack. When storing, separate the
cookies with this paper to prevent them from sticking together.

Lemony & Eggless LemonBars

Bottom Part:
1 Cup unbleached white wheat flour
1/4 Cup powdered sugar
6 Tbs chilled vegan margarine

Top Part:
1 Cup sugar
1/3 C + 2 Tbs soy yogurt
   (plain or lemon flavored)
6 Tbs lemon juice
lemon zest from 1 large lemon
2 Tbs unbleached wheat flour
2 Tbs tapioca flour
2 tsp cornstarch
1/2 tsp baking powder

FIRST: Start with the bottom part. Mix flour and sugar, and then add margarine, cut into bits. Smush it all together with your fingers until it forms a streusel-looking grainy mixture. Line an 8x8 inch pan with parchment paper (bottom + sides), press the bottom layer in nicely, smoothing it flat, and bake it for 15 minutes at 350°F.

SECOND PART:
While the bottom bakes, Mix sugar, soy yogurt and lemon. Whisk together thoroughly.

Mix flours, cornstarch, & baking powder separately before adding them also. Whisk everything together again, mixing very well.

After the bottom has finished its first 15 min. pour the top over it and place back in the oven for 30 minutes at 350°F. Once done, refrigerate to help everything set, and sprinkle the top with powdered sugar!

You likely don't drink all
your recommended 8 cups of
water each day, but c'mon,
give it the old college try!

Though not to be
substituted completely for
our friend "just
water," hot or cold drink
treats can really
hit the spot.

Drinks

NUTTY BANANA SMOOTHIE

1 Cup plain or vanilla soymilk
6 ice cubes
1-2 frozen bananas (depending on size)
1 tsp sugar
2 Tbs peanut butter
2 Tbs chocolate syrup
1 Tbs soy protein powder (optional)
1 Tbs chocolate chips (optional)

– MAKES 2 SERVINGS –

Mix ice with soymilk in a blender until the ice is chopped up.
Cut up the frozen banana(s) into smaller pieces, add, and blend
again. Next, add the peanut butter, sugar, and soy powder –
blend again.
Lastly, blend in the chocolate & chocolate chips.

Try this recipe with other nut butters or grain/nut milks too,
as a variation!

*TIP: Freeze bananas pre-peeled & wrapped in plastic wrap.

ORANGE JULIUS

1 Cup cold water
10-12 ice cubes
1 Cup plain or vanilla ricemilk or soymilk
6 oz frozen orange juice
1 tsp vanilla
1/2 Cup sugar

⟶

First, in a blender, blend the ice cubes with the water and "milk."
Next, add the rest of the ingredients, and blend until the ice
cubes are crushed up thoroughly. Makes 3-4 servings.

Variation: Try this with some vanilla soy or rice ice cream
added too. Yum.

WASSAIL

FOR WINTER

PART ONE

2 1/2 Cups water
3/4 Cup sugar
2 cinnamon sticks
1 1/4 inch thick slice of
   fresh ginger root, peeled
1/2 Tbs whole cloves
1/2 tsp allspice berries <u>or</u>
   1/2 tsp allspice powder

PART TWO

2 Cups orange juice
1/2 Cup lemon juice
1/2 Gallon apple cider (8 Cups)

This is a fancy cider drink that is sometimes made with alcohol — but this one's non-alcoholic. Good treat for holiday gatherings.

First, add together <u>Part I</u> ingredients in a large pot, and bring them to a low boil for 10 minutes. Remove from heat and let sit for up to an hour (to let water soak up the spices).
THEN! add cider, lemon, and orange juices and heat to a low simmer, cooking just until liquid is hot. Once the wassail is nice and hot, serve! ☺

HOT CIDER

1/2 Gallon (= 8 Cups) apple cider
3 Tbs brown sugar
  (or 3 Tbs maple syrup)
1/2 tsp allspice berries
1 tsp whole cloves
2 cinnamon sticks
1/4 tsp salt
1/8 tsp ground nutmeg

(You can use powdered spices if you don't have the whole ones and don't want to take another trip to the store. Halve the allspice and clove amounts and use about 3/4 Tbs for the cinnamon.)

Heat everything at a simmer for about 10-15 minutes (don't boil).
Serve hot, or reheated.

The key to good hot cider is well-soaked spices and enough sweetener. If it's not sweet enough for you, add a little bit more sugar.

Also, as a variation add some orange and lemon zest/peel in with the spices.
(this will change the flavor to resemble wassail.)

fancy
cinnamon - lemon - peppermint tea

12 oz boiling water
1 tea bag of herbal peppermint tea
1 cinnamon stick
2 tsp fresh or bottled lemon juice
2 tsp honey (or use other sweetener, or nothin')

Put everything together in a nice mug and pour in your boiling water. Let steep for about 5 minutes. Remove the cinnamon stick and tea bag, and sip, sip, sip away.

❀ Full of lemony and spicy flavor! ❀
Good for cleaning out greasy feeling, or for softening a cold.
A special change of pace for your peppermint tea.

HOT COCOA

VERSION #1 (To-Go)

12 oz boiling water
Soymilk powder for 1 cup of soymilk
  --> (may vary by brand, but approximately 1/8 to 1/4 Cup)
1 Tbs dutch process cocoa powder
1 Tbs + 2 tsp powdered sugar
    (or 1 Tbs granulated sugar)
dash of salt

* Mix dry ingredients in a 12 oz mug while boiling water. Add water and mix well. This recipe is good for taking on camping trips.

VERSION #2

12 oz soymilk, plain or vanilla
1 Tbs dutch cocoa powder
1 Tbs + 2 tsp powdered sugar
    (or 1 Tbs granulated sugar)
dash of salt
dash of vanilla
1/2 tsp vegan margarine
  or coconut oil

* If using granulated sugar, first run some sugar in a food processor to make the grains smaller.
*Bring soymilk to medium heat in a sauce-pan on the stovetop. Add other ingredients and whisk well. Turn the stove up to get a good simmer, and then turn it back down again and serve.

Variation: Try adding flavored syrup like mint, cherry, etc.

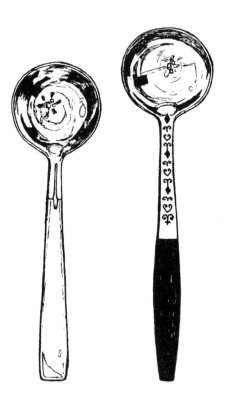

What page was that on?
Are there any recipes with
seitan?
Are there any more
rabbits in this book?

Hey, is this book even about
rabbits?

Recipe Index

ABOUT THE AUTHOR

Beth A. Barnett is sometimes called Beth Bee and lives in a nice little city in Oregon's lush Willamette Valley called Corvallis. Besides writing *Rabbit Food Cookbook*, she also runs the micropress Beth Bee Books, does some freelance illustration, paints oil paintings in a contemporary realism style, and has a job during the day that is completely unrelated to any of that.

Beth has been practicing vegan cooking and baking since 1993, whilst a teenager in Indianapolis, Indiana. She first learned to cook and bake with her mother, Sharon, now of Mt. Pleasant, South Carolina, who likes many of the recipes in *Rabbit Food Cookbook*, and especially the scrambled tofu. To learn more about Beth's work, visit www.bethbee.com.

★